GROUP DYNAMICS
IN THE
RELIGIOUS LIFE

Group Dynamics in the Religious Life

W. W. MEISSNER, S.J.

1965

University of Notre Dame Press

Imprimi Potest: *James J. Shanahan, S.J.*
Provincial of the Buffalo Province

Nihil Obstat: *Joseph Hoffman, C.S.C.*
Censor Deputatus

Imprimatur: *Leo A. Pursley, D.D., L.L.D.*
Bishop of Fort Wayne-South Bend

Copyright 1965 by
University of Notre Dame Press
Notre Dame, Indiana

Library of Congress Catalog Card Number 65-21070

Manufactured in the United States of America
by North State Press, Inc., Hammond, Ind.

CONTENTS

Introduction

Two pressing problems complicate modern religious life. First, vocations have registered a sharp increase, bestowing a blessing that is at the same time liberally sprinkled with difficulties; and secondly, even should the first problem be solved, today's religious functionary faces another grave difficulty, that of being called upon—with ever-increasing urgency and frequency—to perform professional-level tasks. In American religious life these complicating factors have been especially prominent; and as a result, problems in adaptation—unforeseeable only a few decades ago—have become more the rule than the exception.

By itself, a numerical increase in vocations does not bespeak any need for renovation and adaptation. Despite problems such as the forming and training of a whole host of religious recruits, an increase in vocations is generally welcomed by religious groups, who see therein not only a source of vital new life and new blood but also a guarantee that the congregation's work will be carried on.

The matter of the religious functionary's professional status presents more serious questions. Cultural patterns, influenced by the burgeoning scientific movement and other such phenomena, are rapidly changing; new kinds of professional services are being constantly demanded while the value attached to older types diminishes with surprising rapidity. Even within well-defined professional areas, technological progress is demanding new methods and new skills that in themselves require high-level professional training. These demands of progress have made themselves felt most keenly in the very areas—education and hospital work—in which the vast bulk of American religious (92.30 per cent of all females, for example) now work. Not so long ago, teaching communities could rely on the amateur talents of some of their members. Now, an imposing array of high-level standards established by both teachers' groups and accrediting organizations confront the congregations dedicated to educational work. The level of modern education soars ever higher, leaving the teacher with insufficient professional training far in the ruck. The same can be said, with even greater emphasis, for the field of medical science and administration. More than a charitable heart and a willing hand are necessary in modern hospital work. Medical care—and hospital care, in particular—has developed into a highly complex and technical business; consequently, unless medical personnel receive the best in professional preparation, their deficiencies become distressingly obvious all too soon.

Contemporary society has little patience with good intentions that are not translated into action. Instead, it values that which it has every right to expect: professional competence and professional performance. Any group dedicated to providing professional service but failing, in practice, to provide such, quickly discovers that its services go begging. Hence, the pressure on religious groups to adapt to the new and rapidly changing environment has become even more intensified.

Around this rock of adaptation, religious groups flounder—and sometimes they founder, too. Adaptation is no simple matter for them: since religious groups have other purposes than simply rendering professional services, they must do more than arrive at, and then execute, hard but simple decisions. The religious group exists for the perfection and personal sanctification of its members. It has traditions, laws, and customs of its own which comprise its fundamental framework as well as its characteristic way of life. Thus, while adaptation is difficult, its execution is essential to the religious community's continuance.

Seen from this point of view, anything that will help religious to understand the way in which their groups function is likely to speed the process of intelligent adaptation. Studies of religious life are abundant on the theological and canonical levels, but attempts to analyze the life from a scientific standpoint remain relatively few and far between. In sociology, the work of Father Joseph Fichter[1] represents an encouraging beginning. The most substantial analysis from the standpoint of psychology—a field wherein the entries have been relatively few—is that of Father W. C. Bier;[2] but even here the author deals with religious *candidates* rather than with professed religious. While the dearth of scientifically-validated data about the religious life's processes and problems remains a depressing fact, it may well be that before long increasing environmental

---

[1] J. H. Fichter, S.J., "The Sociological Aspects of the Role of Authority in the Adaptation of the Religious Community for the Apostolate," in Joseph E. Haley, C.S.C., ed., *1958 Sisters' Institute of Spirituality* (Notre Dame, Ind.: University of Notre Dame Press, 1959); *Religion as an Occupation* (Notre Dame, Ind.: University of Notre Dame Press, 1961).

[2] W. C. Bier, S.J., "Psychological Testing of Candidates and the Theology of Vocation," *Review for Religious*, XII (1953), 291-304; "Practical Requirements of a Program for the Psychological Screening of Candidates," *Review for Religious*, XIII (1954), 13-27.

pressures will cause this vacuum to be filled. As the need for adaptation becomes ever more acute, readiness to accept aid from sociology, psychology, and psychiatry is likely to register a proportionate increase. From sheer necessity, then, the methods of these sciences, as well as their potential contributions, will be recognized and utilized.

The present study represents an effort to broaden the understanding of religious life by spelling it out in terms of group dynamics. The study called group dynamics is a comparatively youthful offspring of social psychology, but its findings and its methods have already been successfully applied in industry, in education, and in a whole number of other group-related activities. The principles of group functioning discovered by students of group dynamics appear equally applicable to the functioning of religious communities. The present study begins from this premise.

Caution, however, must be exercised. The religious group is not just any group, as we shall see. It has peculiarities of structure which even on a strictly scientific basis render it distinct from other groups. Moreover, the life of the religious group is not governed solely by the action and interaction of human agents. Since its major purpose is engagement in and commitment to the praise, service, and love of God, the religious life necessarily focuses its attention on God and the things of God; it is a life in which Grace plays a major role. From the standpoint of scientific inquiry, which the present study plans to follow, this spiritual aspect will not be considered as such. Yet, since the supernatural dimension is an ever-present and active reality in the life of the religious group, neither can it be ignored. Its presence underlines the need for caution in applying some of the scientific findings to the religious group.

Even while such an undertaking demands scrupulous care, the basic validity of its approach must be granted. If we are theologically correct in asserting that Grace does not inhibit the actions of natural agents, we may further assert that an understanding of the religious group's life demands an understanding of that group's characteristic processes. The life of the group cannot be adequately grasped merely in terms of the personal traits of its individual members, nor even in terms of interaction between this and that set of numbers. The group itself provides a broader context of understanding without which other aspects remain undefined and unexplained. In this study, attention will be focused specifically on the group itself, its processes, and its functions.

Therefore, what is being undertaken here is neither a sociological nor a psychological analysis. At a number of points, the dynamics of the group and the dynamics of the individual will interact, and on such occasions problems relating to personality development or functioning may be touched on tangentially. But the prime interest and intent will always remain with the group as such.

We have deliberately limited our analysis to the synthesizing of current experimental conclusions about group dynamics, and then, to applying these conclusions to various aspects of religious group functioning. As a result, we have refrained from making specific evaluations or criticisms of traditional practices and customs. Two significant reasons have dictated our approach in this matter: first, while group dynamics has

successfully explained many of the ordinary mechanisms of group functioning, the pertinence of its principles is difficult to ascertain without studying directly
all the relevant factors of particular cases; secondly,
the study of group dynamics has revealed that the
balance between fundamental tendencies differs for
each group studied (see Chapter 2), and thus, judgments about specific group practices cannot be made
unless consideration is given to the relationship between the specified practice and the group's typical
culture. The aim of this investigation, therefore, will
be directed at the more general and broader category
of attitudes and principles. Occasionally, extremes that
run counter to the findings of group dynamics (and to
the best interests of any group, as well) will be indicated. These, however, will be seen as merely the exceptions that·prove the rule.

Very little in these pages will offer new information
to the wide-ranging reader. Any person familiar with
the religious life will also be familiar with the facts
presented here. Our hope, however, is to set these
familiar facts within a new frame of reference. Thus
will all those areas of interaction capable of influencing
the reactions of individual religious—not to mention the
reactions of the group itself—emerge squarely in the
forefront of the stage of understanding, far from their
present shadowy locations in its wings.

1

The Religious Community
As A Group

Before embarking on a detailed consideration of group processes within the religious community, one must seek to determine what it is that constitutes the "religious community" and, further, what characteristics distinguish this community as a type of group. Although the religious community possesses qualities and characteristics that make it distinct from other groups, many of its structures and functions are common to any organized group. The extent to which experimental findings and conclusions may be validly applied to the religious group will depend on the degree to which the characteristics of the experimental and religious groups coincide. Whenever and to whatever extent these characteristics diverge, care must be taken in making analogies and interpreting the processes of the religious community.

Therefore, we must begin our study by analyzing the religious group itself. Only in this way can its position with respect to the descriptive categories of group dynamics be definitively established. Even though a *complete* understanding of the religious group's characteristics hinges on the grasping of certain technical concepts, a start can be made by determining a general classification for the religious group and then proceeding to an examination of the specific characteristics that help to make it *this* rather than *that* type.

A "group" may be defined in several ways. If it is understood as a plurality of persons, within a particular context, interacting with one another more than with other persons, it can designate two people playing gin rummy or a nation of millions. To clarify, it will help to distinguish between "primary" and "secondary" groups. Primary refers to those groups in which individuals interact in face-to-face relationships, a description that in itself limits the size of such groups. In the secondary group, the members' relationships are indirect and—frequently, simply because of the great numbers involved—assume a more structured and organized form. The example of a large city makes the difference between the two kinds of group readily apparent: in the urban condition, contact between citizens has more of the secondary group's characteristics, since it is largely indirect; it takes place by means of interaction within the city's organized structure rather than in the face-to-face, or primary, manner. At the same time, of course, subgroups that are primary in nature, families, for example, are numerous in cities, too. Yet membership in the urban group does not, in general, involve the direct relations experienced in primary groups. The generalization that may be drawn is that the secondary group tends to form itself artificially, whereas the primary group is more apt to be a naturally functioning kind of organization.

This distinction between primary and secondary groups is important simply because the types of processes occurring within each group are so different. Whereas the secondary group is more disposed to emphasize administration and to regard members as all cut from the same cloth, the primary group tends to function in a converse manner. One problem that arises in classifying groups is the difficulty—if not the downright impossibility—of drawing a clear line of demarcation between primary and secondary. How large, for instance, must a group become before it loses the characteristic of direct relationships? Primary and secondary are probably best explained as abstract terms used to deal with what is in reality a continuum of group types.

A group is not merely a collection of people. Its functions and goals constitute its attraction for others, and it is the unity of purpose and participation by its members in a common activity that lend it its organic character. The group is more than a logical category, possessing, as it does, an organization and a function that the logical category does not have. More specifically, the group consists of a number of particular agents who have chosen to belong to this group and to participate in its activities in certain ways and under certain conditions.

To situate the religious group definitively in this type of analysis is difficult, to say the least. Immediately and proximately, the religious community is that group in which the individual religious lives and works. At this level, the religious community clearly exhibits the traits of a primary group. At the same time, the local religious community is a functioning part of a larger group that we call the congregation or the order. This latter level of organization falls under the classification of secondary group. It is impossible to consider the local community in isolation from its parent congregation—particularly when the larger organization is so intimately connected with and exercises such influence over the smaller one that the group processess tend to interact and overlap. In the local community, the process will for the most part be along primary lines; yet influences stemming from higher superiors, the secondary group structure, will strongly affect the primary group's operations. Thus, in any analysis, it will not suffice to classify the local religious community as *simply* a primary group.

A number of factors affect the determination of the type of a particular group. Among these are size, amount of physical interaction among members, degree of intimacy, level of solidarity, locus of control over group activities, extent of formalization of the rules, and the tendency of members to react to one another either as individuals or as players of certain roles.[1]

Local religious communities vary considerably in size, from the two or three members in a parish or a retreat house to the large seminaries where several hundred may dwell in community. In smaller religious communities the primary quality of the group is easily maintained, and as a consequence interpersonal relations play a much greater part in the group's functioning. As might be expected, the influence of interpersonal relations on group life decreases in importance as the size of the community increases. Correlatively, within these larger groups there is apt to be greater reliance on impersonal and formal administrative pro-

---

[1] D. Cartwright and A. Zander, "Issues and Basic Assumptions," in Cartwright and Zander, eds., *Group Dynamics* (Evanston, Ill.: Row, Peterson, 1953), pp. 33-65.

cedures. Insofar as the common activities of the larger community encourage face-to-face interaction, the group retains its primary character. It is a fact, though, that such large communities cannot be accurately classified as either primary or secondary.

The amount of physical interaction among members also varies markedly. Size is obviously influential here, since the physical interaction among members of a small community is much more frequent and covers a broader range of activities than would be possible in a large community. Subgroupings based on shared interests, friendship, and participation in the same activities are sure to arise in any community, and hence the amount of interaction with other members varies according to each individual's inclination. In principle, however, and according to that virtue of charity that not only guides religious life but also is given legal form in each congregation's rules, physical interaction is to extend to every member. The only exception to this principle lies in the distinction of "grades" within the religious order, whereby members are divided into categories, on each of which are bestowed specific functions and characteristics.

An example of this may be found in the distinction between Brothers and priests in some religious orders. To some extent, too, law or custom may regulate the relationships between members of these grades. Although charity still furnishes the over-all guiding norm, relationships among members of different grades remain qualitatively different from relationships among members of the same grade. Physical interaction will also depend on the nature of the individual member's work, as well as on the kind of objectives the com-

munity is seeking. It is obvious that the physical interaction of a nun who teaches all day in school will differ
from that of a nun who carries on her work in a con-
vent. Again, life in a community devoted to apostolic
works, *extra muros,* is bound to differ from one in
which members almost always adhere to communal
life.

Members of a religious community enjoy a rather
high degree of intimacy, a natural outgrowth of the
closeness of community life and the sharing of mutual
values, ideals, and attitudes. Any primary group, by its
very structure, encourages informality and familiarity in
relations among group members; however, the religious
community generally strives to restrain this tendency,
encouraging instead a certain atmosphere of formality
and mutual respect. The religious group's reasoning follows this line: formality and mutual respect are helpful
in fostering an appreciation of the dignity of each member of the group as a religious consecrated to God's
service. Moreover, the ideal of charity is more likely to
be achieved in an atmosphere of dignified reserve than
in one of overfamiliarity, wherein some members of
the community might be overlooked in the normal practice of charity. The same argument may be used with
respect to group solidarity: if members' relationships
follow a certain uniform pattern, attachment to the
group's objectives and functions will not be lost sight
of. The need for striking a balance between warm interpersonal relations and group solidarity is thus quite
plain.[2]

---

[2] J. H. Fichter, S.J., "The Sociological Aspects of the Role of Authority
in the Adaptation of the Religious Community for the Apostolate," in
Joseph E. Haley, C.S.C., ed., *1958 Sisters' Institute of Spirituality*
(Notre Dame, Ind.: University of Notre Dame Press, 1959), p. 42.

Solidarity itself is ideally, if not always actually, of the greatest importance in the religious community. Members have freely and totally dedicated their lives to the order or congregation to which they belong. They have chosen to find their self-fulfillment and, ultimately, their spiritual enrichment and salvation in this particular order. They have committed themselves to the attainment of perfection according to the pattern laid down in their institute's formal rule. The life of the group and participation in its activities thereby assume a centrality that would be difficult to duplicate in any other way; it is not only expected but more or less required that the individual member accept and cling to the group's values and that his personal activity be joined with that of his comrades toward the achievement of group goals.

These group goals exist on two levels. The first and more general level consists of the goals placed before each individual as a member of the larger organization, the order or the congregation. Such goals are broad and somewhat loosely defined, but they are powerful in shaping the character of group activity at every level. Each order, each institute, has a specific character, more or less distinctive, that can be expressed in terms of the organization's "spirit." This specific character of the group's goals plays a major role in persuading members to undertake one set of apostolic works in preference to another, in inculcating certain types of religious practice rather than others, or in stressing one facet of Christian spirituality instead of another. Often these characteristics have been handed down from the order's founder, and time has given them a special aura.

Take the Jesuits, Dominicans, Benedictines, Franciscans, and Carthusians, for example. Each order possesses a quality peculiar to itself; each dedicates itself to a special apostolic and spiritual ideal that can be justly called Ignatian, Franciscan, Benedictine, and so on. Sometimes a single quality incorporating the impression given by the community can be spelled out concretely: Jesuit obedience, Franciscan poverty, Dominican preaching, Carthusian contemplation. Particular apostolic works, such as teaching, hospital and charitable works, and preaching, may become so identified with a community that they attain the status of a group goal.

Within the large, over-all religious organization—within its broad aims—each individual community has more specific goals that are characteristic of its functions and duties. A seminary instructor is interested in religious formation; religious attached to a school or university have educational aims; parish priests work toward a set of pastoral goals; nuns in charge of a hospital specify their concrete goals within a general context of charity. As each religious dedicates himself or herself to these goals, solidarity achieves its central position in the life of the community. The answers to such questions do indicate how harmoniously the group functions, how much personal fulfillment is achieved by individual members, how highly members value the group's activities, how much they esteem its goals, and how actively they are participating in the attainment of these.

There is never doubt in religious communities as to who controls the group's activities. A clearly defined hierarchy extends from the highest authority, the "general," down to the group's lowest stratum, the "rank-and file" member. Within the local community there is always a superior whose authority is supreme at that level and who, in turn, is subject to the organization's next higher authority. Canon law and the organization's own rule make explicit the extent of the authority at each level. Each official has jurisdiction over certain matters: the local superior can grant some permissions but must defer others to the provincial; the provincial is similarly limited, being required to turn over specific questions to the general; and the same is true even of the general, whose powers are limited by the general chapter and, of course, by the Church itself as the final arbiter. The impact of these various levels of authority tends to modify both the structure and function of the local community and the activity of each member. A bureaucratic emphasis, embodying the well-known approach through channels, is thus imposed, and distance separates the locus of authority from the rank-and-file member. Certain values and attitudes that would be absent from a more informal organization are introduced; yet the organization does not become wholly rigid since the bureaucratic tendency is modified by many other factors.

Nearly every religious group has a set of rules governing relations among its members. The nature of activities, for instance, is usually heavily circumscribed, as well as the time and place in which they may be indulged. The community almost always has a daily schedule that at least prescribes the times for such community exercises as Mass, prayer in common, meals, and recreation. The prescriptions are frequently more detailed and may cover most of the day's activities.

Some time is always made available for the individual's personal needs and interests, but unrestricted social interaction with other members of the community is confined to stated recreation periods. Such periods usually follow the noon and evening meals and last for one half-hour or more. Then the religious turns to the next prescribed duty.

A further limit on the amount of social interaction among members is imposed by the community's rule of silence. In contemplative communities, in which silence is an essential part of the prayer life, the rule is followed rigorously, but even among members of actively apostolic groups, only brief, passing conversations and communications necessary to carry on everyday activities are permitted. Unnecessary noise and talking are always avoided. Thus the communications between members of the group are limited both quantitatively and qualitatively. This restriction, when added to the intimacy that characterizes relationships in any religious community, produces a unique atmosphere of personal interaction.

The last basic element in defining a group type is the tendency of members to react to one another either as individuals or as players of roles. The fact is that in religious groups members definitely tend to react to each other as persons. The whole structure of religious life, founded as it is on charity, fosters in every member a keen appreciation of the personal dignity of each fellow religious. Although religious relationships may be more formal than affectionate, they always remain distinctively personal. Some groups insist on the use of proper titles, such as Sister, Father, or Brother, whereas others permit a more familiar address. The former practice safeguards formality and the latter encourages familiarity, but the difference is only a matter of degree.

It is evident that the religious community is a somewhat complex sociocultural system.[3] It is organized along both familial and communal lines, and it is this dual organization that largely determines its members' daily activities. Within the larger context of the order, wherein authority is the hallmark, a more bureaucratic form of organization prevails. Unique personal and apostolic goals lend both the individual religious community and the over-all organization a special character that no other type of group can duplicate.

The religious community is a variety of familial-communal, bureaucratic, and professional organizations all in one, which must, nevertheless, be analyzed as a whole. The opposition among these characteristics makes the task of evaluation even more difficult. For example, a familial kind of organization operates on different premises and predicates different expectations of its members' roles than a bureaucratic organization would. And likewise, a bureaucratic structure's values and demands are strongly opposed to the values and demands of professional activity.[4] Yet, despite the opposition among the various aspects of religious community life, the group *must* integrate these conflicting aspects into a harmonious whole if its goals are to be attained.

The religious community obviously differs from a family. All its members are of the same sex; there is no reproductive function; since members are adults there is no question of educating or training children. In

---

[3] *Ibid.*, pp. 35-42.
[4] P. M. Blau and W. R. Scott, *Formal Organizations: A Comparative Approach* (San Francisco: Chandler, 1962), pp. 60-74.

many other ways the religious community may be considered as analogous to the family. Formal titles of familial origin, like Mother, Father, Sister, and Brother, are bestowed upon members, and the superior's role is often likened to that of a parent. The very notion of the religious group as a family implies a certain identification of one member with another, a sense of intimacy and familiarity, a mutuality of concerns and activities, a common economic foundation, a sharing of each other's burdens, and the sustenance of members on many levels, including the satisfaction of such basic needs as food and sleep. Fichter[5] has summarized the characteristics common to the religious community and the familial-communal type of organization:

> (1) relatively small number of members; (2) frequent face-to-face relations and primary contacts among members; (3) relatively permanent location permitting the identification of the group even though some of the personnel may change from time to time; (4) a sense of solidarity and loyalty to the group; (5) a consensus of values in which the members share basic ideals; (6) patterns of behavior that are stable and tend to change very slowly.

Later, we will attempt to study some of the more important aspects of group life in the religious community, and we will try to trace some of the lines of influence of this specific kind of group process on the psychological adjustment of individual members. Even if we accept, as a common-sense appraisal, the judgment that personality profoundly influences group functioning and, conversely, that group structure and function help

---

[5] Fichter, "The Sociological Aspects . . . ," in Haley, *op. cit.*, pp. 37-38.

shape the individual religious, our task remains difficult.

Our approach will be broadly empirical in the sense that we will devote our attention more to the patterns of interaction that develop within the religious community's primary associations than to the formal statements of the community's norms embodied in the rules. Since we do not possess a sufficiently large body of empirical evidence that has been scientifically validated or even obtained through direct examination, our research labors under a serious handicap. Because of the difficulties involved in obtaining this kind of information, we are forced to rely to a considerable degree on empirical studies conducted on other types of groups. We shall attempt to apply the discoveries in these other fields to the religious group, basing our inferences primarily on personal observation.

Like participant observation, personal observation has definite limitations, but it has definite merits as well, especially when circumstances negate the use of more objective methods. We have tried to broaden the base of experience by an informal exchange of views with other religious; this exchange of views, although helpful in correcting and modifying personal observations, cannot take the place of a more direct and objective study of the group process. Consequently, it is by no means certain that findings based on other types of groups can be validly applied to the religious group. Keeping in mind the unique nature of the religious group will serve as a reminder that our conclusions may well bear qualification.

Let us not be overcautious, however. The religious community does affect and is affected by group processes. The formal study of group interaction presumes that there are some generalized group processes and interactions that are discernible in any group. The religious community, as a group, can be regarded as subject to the general laws of group functioning. The information accumulated in the study of group dynamics, with its profound insights into the operation of human groups, can shed light on the way the religious group functions. If our understanding of the nature of religious life is deepened by this examination of its group aspects, we can at least hope that a more intelligent and better integrated religious life will result. Since the religious community exists for the perfection and sanctification of its members, it must necessarily place a high premium on each member's personal fulfillment and on the most productive and rewarding interaction possible among members. Neither of these goals is achievable without an awareness of that group which plays a dominant part in the life of every religious community.

Once again, it should be realized that classification of the religious group's characteristics is a difficult task. The religious group does not fit neatly into any clear-cut category of group process yet conceptualized. It is a unique kind of group, blending in its own specific way those qualities and dimensions that identify the structure of any group. At the same time, the religious community does possess a group structure and does perform definite group functions. In the next chapter we will study the basic elements of the group process that might be encountered in any type of group. Once we have grasped these fundamental elements, we can proceed to explore in greater detail the group process and group life as they relate to the religious community.

2

The Group Process

The scientific study of groups as groups is of fairly recent origin. Well-established data relevant to the broad, over-all spectrum of group activities are simply not available in any great quantity. Research is hampered by the absence of any single dominant theory of group activity, the presence of which would lend a decisive direction to thinking about groups and their functions. For these reasons, a fully systematic picture of the nature of a group and its operations cannot yet be presented. Instead, a somewhat fragmentary picture, only now emerging from partial data and incomplete concepts, must suffice.

The reasons why people belong to groups and engage in group activities are complex. The complexity of motivation that applies generally applies equally to membership and participation in religious groups. Superficially, however, it can be maintained that a member considers a group attractive because it presents him with an opportunity either to achieve some sort of personal reward or to avoid some kind of punishment or pain. The "centrality" of a member's position within a group is closely related to reward and punishment. The greater the esteem in which a member is held by the group, the

15

more influence he will exercise, the more adequacy he will demonstrate in the group situation, the more support he will receive from other members of the group, and the more" central" will be his position within the group. To sum up, in group life a member is rewarded when he moves into a more central position, and he is punished when he is pushed into a position on the group's periphery.

Basic to an understanding of the nature of the group process is identification. Individuals identify with one another because of ties to one or another central person, or because of shared interests and purposes, or because of common emotional needs. The ties that bind the group together are multiple, but it is a mark of the group process that members consider them as proper to the group as a whole. Consequently, the interaction and communication among members give rise to a set of agreements, shared values, perceptions and expectations, and in particular to a set of common goals; these in their totality constitute the group's "culture." This culture, since it reflects the needs and desires of individual members, promotes and intensifies the sense of identification members feel toward the group.

The group exists for two basic reasons, one psychological and the other social. Psychologically, the group satisfies individual personality needs. Socially, the group reflects a shared desire to effect some alteration in the environment, either physical or social. Of prime interest to the religious group are changes in the social environment, but changes that are incidentally physical, such as building colleges, hospitals, and so on, must also be included. When the group functions as a "psyche-group," that is, when it acts primarily in terms of internal demands, its psychological goals are more readily achieved. On the other hand, the group achieves its social goals more quickly when it is organized to meet demands seen as external to it. In this mode of operating, it is acting as a "socio-group."

The dual character of group organization—psychic and social—may be expressed in various ways. In addition to the distinction between psyche-group and socio-group made by Jennings,[1] Homans has clarified the difference between an "external" and "internal" system,[2] and Bion has distinguished between "tendencies toward emotionality" and "tendencies toward work."[3] As Thelen[4] has pointed out, these dual characteristics cannot be regarded as equal to one another, but they do indicate the group's basic duality so far as its being "inner-" and "outer-directed."[5] Thus the fundamental problem of group functioning is to find a way to satisfy, harmoniously and effectively, both the personality needs of

---

[1] H. H. Jennings, "Sociometric Differentiation of the Psyche-Group and the Socio-Group," *Sociometry*, X (1947), 71-79.

[2] G. C. Homans, *The Human Group* (New York: Harcourt, Brace, 1950).

[3] W. R. Bion, *Experiences in Groups* (New York: Basic Books, 1961). Bion's work was originally published as a series of articles in *Human Relations*, 1948-1951.

[4] H. A. Thelen, "Work-Emotionality Theory of the Group as Organism," in S. Koch, ed., *Psychology: A Study of a Science* (New York: McGraw-Hill, 1959), III, 544-611.

[5] The use of inner-directed and outer-directed in this context should be distinguished from the well-known application of these terms by David Riesman in *The Lonely Crowd* (New Haven: Yale University Press, 1950). Riesman's terms are applied to the functioning of the individual personality, whereas the present usage refers to processes proper to the group as such. The functions of the group are inner-directed insofar as they are primarily concerned with relations among members within the group. They are outer-directed insofar as they are primarily concerned with relations between the group and its environment.

group members and the demands of its environmental goals.

Because a group possesses the dual traits of inner- and outer-directedness, the possibility of conflict, tension, anxiety, ambiguity, and confusion is always present. Whenever this possibility becomes actuality, the need to reconcile and harmonize the warring elements arises. The twin motivations underlying this need for reconciliation are by no means obscure: the individual requires the security that only order can bestow, and for the group to attain its external environmental goals, its resources must be organized to the utmost efficiency.

Whenever reconciliation is required, however, a new pattern is created among the warring elements. The very effort to harmonize, or reconcile, gives rise to shifts in centrality, alterations in group structure, activation of formerly latent personal needs, new patterns of interpersonal interaction, redefinition of purposes and objectives, and new externally directed functions. All of these changes reorganize and redefine the group culture, and the ensuing reorganization brings new patterns of inner- and outer-directedness that demand further reconciliation and harmonization. To understand the group process, then, one must conceive of it in dynamic terms, since the group constantly evolves and alters.

The process of change can take place within a group both consciously and unconsciously. On the conscious level, intelligence may be used to analyze and correct disturbing conditions. Objective external conditions are usually conceived of in a partially conscious manner and can thus be dealt with by direct action.[6] The

---

[6] Thelen, "Work-Emotionality . . .," in Koch, *op. cit.*

group's conscious direction toward publicly stated goals and the organization of its activities for their achievement are among the fundamental dimensions of the group process. In fact, these external demands are those that are consciously perceived as primary; the group's internal structure must accommodate itself to these, and not vice versa. On the unconscious level, however, the situation is reversed. So far as motivation, identification, position, and so on are concerned, problems relevant to the inner system hold the primary place of influence. From this point of view, the external task-oriented operation is considered merely as providing a medium for higher priority, emotionalized human purposes.

Thus, the group can be understood as a system composed of individual personalities acting as subsystems and operating within a given environmental context. By means of group culture, the social system is able to exert a certain control over the actions and interactions of the group's individual personalities. To divert its activity toward external problems, the group must bring to bear certain kinds of actions according to the conditions and nature of the problem. The group must reorganize itself internally so that the necessary roles can be developed and resources of group members mobilized effectively. As Bion observed, a group has two basic tendencies, "work" and "emotionality." Since a group is always engaged in some kind or degree of work, strain on one or another part of the system is inevitable. Responsive strains develop in other parts of the same system and, depending on the system's properties, may be transmitted throughout the whole. Bion describes the primary property of the group system as a "basic assumption of group purpose or need," and it is his conviction that the entire culture of the group is eventually organized around this assumption.

The basic distinction between tendencies to work and tendencies to emotionality in the functioning of the group can be illuminated to a certain extent by relating them to more concrete patterns of behavioral interaction within the group. A set of categories for the analysis of interaction in small groups has been provided by Bales[7] and has been reproduced in this chapter. Paralleling Bion's distinction between work and emotionality, Bales divides the areas of interaction into "task" and "emotional" areas. Task areas are conceptualized in terms of questions and answers; emotional areas are conceptualized as either positive or negative. Problems of orientation, evaluation, and control are regarded as related primarily to the task area; problems of decision, tension management, and integration are considered related to the emotional area. Decision as it is used here does not refer to decision-making, but rather to decision-accepting. Decision-making would belong under orientation or control. It is immediately obvious that these categories do not provide an exhaustive system of analysis. They do help to spell out the kinds of activity we are referring to when we speak of work or emotionality.

Emotionality, then, is an inner-directed, primitive, unlearned response of the group to unconscious needs to maintain itself under the pressure of strain, which may derive from sources external or internal to the

[7] R. F. Bales, "A Set of Categories for the Analysis of Small Group Interaction," *American Sociological Review,* XV (1950), 257-63. See also Bales, *Interaction Process Analysis* (Cambridge, Mass.: Addison-Wesley, 1950).

R. F. Bales's Chart of Categories

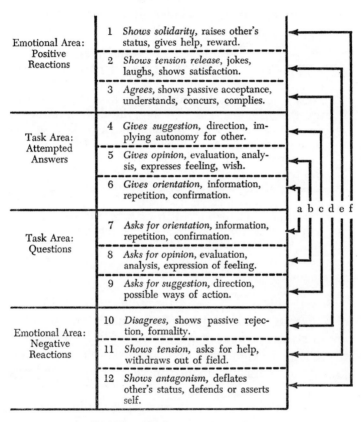

Key:

a — Problems of orientation
b — Problems of evaluation
c — Problems of control
d — Problems of decision
e — Problems of tension management
f — Problems of integration

group. The basic assumptions are patterns of emotionality that dominate the group interaction. Bion originally described three such basic patterns, fight-flight, dependency, and pairing.[8] Thelen describes the basic assumptions, synthetically, as follows:

> Fight is any expression of aggression toward the prob-
> lem, the group, an outside agency, the leader, the self,
> or anything else. Flight is any behavior of "running
> away" from stress by such means as joking, breaking
> up the meeting, daydreaming, incoherent rambling
> discussion, "academic" presentation, etc. Dependency
> is shown in any behavior which seeks aid from outside
> the person: from the leader, the minutes of the last
> meeting, traditions, experts, and so on. Usually such
> seeking of aid is accompanied by expressions of weak-
> ness and inadequacy: "the job is too big," "we don't
> have the resources," etc. Pairing behavior includes inti-
> mate remarks made privately to another individual,
> "reaching out" to others with expression of warmth, ap-
> proval, or agreement, or even by extension, a warm
> statement to the group.[9]

Although this description is formulated in terms of discussion groups, the dynamics are characteristic of the
group structure as such and can readily be applied to
the religious community. Fight, for example, is often expressed in complaint about superiors or about the way
in which community projects are conducted. As such,
it is a form of emotionality operating within the community's group system. Thelen also breaks down Bion's
concept of work into four categories: individual work;
group housekeeping, in which the group makes routine

---

[8] W. R. Bion, "Experiences in Groups: III," *Human Relations,* II
(1949), 13-22.
[9] Thelen, "Work Emotionality . . .," in Koch, *op. cit.,* p. 578.

decisions about its own operations; task- or goal-directed work; and integrative work, in which the effort is made to relate what the group is doing to the kind of group it wants to be.

The group system, with its dynamically shifting arrangement of work-emotionality characteristics, exercises control over the interactions among members and lends these interactions a discernible pattern and sequence that continually shift from one arrangement of the basic assumptions to another in each successive phase of the group process. The stress situations to which the group is subjected create demands and tensions for its individual members. The response of members seeking to reduce tension can take the direct form of acting-out. If the individual is threatened, the acting-out may translate this impulsive response to stress into patterns of behavior that will yield varying consequences according to the pattern the acting-out follows. Pairing increases the capacity to cope with the threat without actually diminishing it. Dependency neither increases nor decreases nor removes the threat; it relies on the support derived from the object of dependence. Fight can wipe out the source of the threat, but not without considerable disturbance on all fronts. Flight removes the subject from the threat without increasing his capacity to deal with it. All of these patterns of response to stress are nonadaptive, insofar as the acting-out is impulsive and emotional, and they do not contribute to the individual's capacity to profit from the experience.

There is an alternative mode of response in which the impulsive response is blocked and behavior is mediated by thought processes. Through such processes the nature of threat is diagnosed and analyzed, previous experience is brought to bear, and alternative courses of action are formulated and evaluated. This pattern of response has been designated as "inquiry."[10] Inquiry and acting out are basic modes of response, which can be discerned in all human responses; spontaneous and involuntary expression of impulse blends with the development of awareness of experiential elements and with the capacity to apply what is learned in the process of adaptation. Within the group, acting-out is nonadaptive and tends to build stress; inquiry, on the other hand, tends to be adaptive and reduces tensions. The amount of change that the group can effect and the amount of growth that can be realized within the group depend on the extent to which the energies of the group can be channelled into the inquiry components of the adaptive process.

There is, therefore, a line of continuous influence linking the personal needs of individual members to the culture of the entire group. The stresses arising within the group will trigger responses in the individual that reflect the patterning of needs and expectations peculiar to him. Following Bion's theory, in any group there will be other members who tend to follow a similar mode of adaptation, so that in response to stress subgroups begin to emerge within the group, each pursuing a specific modality for the discharge of tension. Bion characterizes each such modality by a given arrangement or combination of the elements of fight, flight, dependency, pairing, and one or another pattern of work. At any given phase of the group process the preferred mode of adaptation of the dominant

10 *Ibid.*

subgroup becomes the basic assumption of the group, and it is this basic assumption that determines the group culture for that particular phase. Individual members unconsciously identify with one or another subgroup that is engaged in maintaining or promoting a particular basic assumption. The persistence of the basic assumption of participating subgroups within the culture helps explain the dynamic and shifting character of the group culture, which can alter its basic assumption from time to time under varying external and internal stresses. As circumstances change, one subgroup succeeds in getting its basic assumption accepted by the majority, thereby effectively changing the basic assumption of the group.

If we accept this theory as a general framework for consideration of the group process, there are particular aspects of group activity upon which it is important to focus. The external task-orientation of a group is determined by the group goal, and the group goal, operating through the group culture, has a steering effect on the activities of the group members. But it is not always clear that members accept group goals as their own personal goals. The member can influence the group to move it toward a goal congruent with his personal goal. Experimental findings seem to indicate[11] that there is no determinable relation between the difficulty of the goal that the group proposes to the member and the level of aspiration of that member. When the group put stronger pressures on the members to attain a given goal, the members responded by setting a

---

[11] A. Zander, T. Natsoulas, and E. J. Thomas, "Personal Goals and the Group's Goals for the Member," *Human Relations*, XIII (1960), 333-34.

higher level of achievement. And when the goal was difficult, strong pressures brought the members' personal goals more in line with the group goal. But this was not the case when the group goal was relatively easy. Members who set their own level of aspiration closer to the group goal displayed greater attraction to the group and greater involvement in group activity, and they tended to set higher goals for the group. They also showed a greater desire to achieve the level of aspiration they had set for themselves. These members also tended to internalize the group goal more frequently than members whose level of aspiration was less congruent with the group goal. Among members with stronger personal aspiration, there was an inverse relation between the strength of pressures the group brought to bear on them and their rate of production: those exposed to weak pressures tended to produce more than those exposed to strong pressures.

The group member with a high degree of personal aspiration apparently tends more to independence from the group and consequently directs a certain amount of energy to opposing group pressures. For the religious community, this would seem to indicate that strong pressures brought on individuals with a high level of aspiration reinforce a pattern of opposition, the basic modality of fight. Moreover, one might suggest that pressures exerted on members of the religious group to achieve more difficult goals (personal sanctification, apostolic efficiency, and so on) can attain congruence between personal and group goals more readily than pressures exerted to achieve less difficult goals. Unquestionably, the value members attach to these respective goals is an important variable, so that pressures to reinforce observance of minutiae may be expected to enjoy less success than pressures toward more valued goals.

Actually, the setting of group goals is part and parcel of the group's process of adaptive orientation. Group goals are not defined once and for all, as though they were static constants of the group process. Rather, they can be conceived as products of a dynamic and purposeful adaptation that continues operating within the group process and by which the group adapts itself to its environment and to the other groups and social institutions with which it must interact.[12] The change, either in the environment or the organization of the group, requires revision of goals.

Even where the goals of a group are formally stated and fixed, as in religious organizations, the process of applying the formal prescriptions requires interpretation and redefinition when changes occur in either environment or organization. The more unstable the environment, the more critical the problem becomes. Where the measurement and evaluation of the services rendered by an organization are fairly easy, the process of adaptation and readjustment of goals is readily accomplished. But in the religious group, where the services are more intangible and their effectiveness correspondingly more difficult to determine, adaptation and readjustment of goals may prove more difficult.

The whole area of adaptation is a difficult and pressing one for the modern religious group. The religious community is in a peculiar position even when the

---

[12] J. D. Thompson and W. J. McEwen, "Organizational Goals and Environment: Goal-setting as an Interaction Process," *American Sociological Review*, XXIII (1958), 23-31.

goal-setting and goal-modifying decision processes within the group are functioning efficiently. The religious group cannot respond unreservedly to the demands of its social environment, since the group does not exist exclusively for these social goals. The goals of every religious group also, and even primarily, include personal goals related to the life of religious perfection and the exercises of the spiritual life. Consequently, although the goal structure of the religious group can be modified to a degree, parts of it cannot be altered without complete alteration of the nature and purpose of the group. In our own day there has been considerable discussion of the question of what can and should be changed in the goals and modes of operation of the religious group. A perceptive listing of inalterable and alterable elements has been provided by Gallen.[13] Elements which cannot be changed are:

1. The general purpose of the religious life of complete evangelical perfection.

2. The three religious vows and their essential objects, purpose, and spirit.

3. The mortification and prayer necessary for the attainment of the purpose of the religious life.

4. Anything commanded or forbidden by the law of the Church.

5. The distinctive and solid spirit of the particular institute.

6. Anything certainly essential in the institute.
Other elements, which may provide material for change and adaptation, are:

---

[13] J. F. Gallen, "Renovation and Adaptation," *Review for Religious,* XIV (1955), 293-318.

1. Greater care in the admission of candidates and more decisiveness in the early elimination of the unsuitable before perpetual profession.

2. The establishment of a juniorate for Sisters immediately after the noviceship, in which the young professed will complete their undergraduate education or training and continue their spiritual formation.

3. A sounder doctrinal formation in the postulancy, noviceship, and juniorate.

4. The elimination of prominent externalism and formalism.

5. Proper concept of the founder or foundress.

6 Greater attention to the purpose and spirit of the vows rather than to their mere obligation.

7. A schedule of prayer that gives proper emphasis to mental prayer, is sufficiently liturgical, and is not excessive in the quantity or the importance placed on vocal prayer.

8. Direction of the works of the institute to the needs of our time, which in most institutes will consist of an emphasis on works for the poor and the working class.

9. A horarium (time order) that is less contributory to tension and that provides for proper daily, weekly, and annual rest.

10. Greater care in the selection of and, if possible, previous training for local superiors and novice masters and mistresses.

11. A government that is more spiritual, individual, paternal or maternal, and embodying the necessary firmness.

12. Establishment of a tertianship and, perhaps, of a period of recollection before perpetual profession.

13. Greater emphasis on maturity, a sense of responsibility, dependability, efficiency, and proper initiative in the training of religious.

14. Simplification of the religious habit.

15. Higher intellectual standards in continued study and preparation for classes.

16. Elimination of the continued rotation of the same superiors.

17. Greater mutual knowledge of, cooperation with, and attention to the interests of other religious institutes.

18. Possible extension of the period of temporary vows to five years.

The list is a long one and could easily be extended. The items subject to change represent pressing areas of adjustment that environmental demands from a constantly changing social and cultural world are forcing religious groups to face.[14]

This continuing and necessary interaction between the group and its environment introduces an element of environmental control, that is, the control exercised by the social environment on the group's functioning and decision processes. Regardless of the professed objectives of the religious group (salvation of souls, teaching, hospital work), it is essential for its continued ope-

---

[14] Gallen's list of elements for adaptation in religious groups is not a listing of goals to which the religious group can or should direct itself. Rather it is a partial catalogue of areas of adaptation that may be called for because of the shifting goal-orientation of the religious group in contemporary culture.

ration that it produce some service of value to the environment. Thompson and McEwen[15] have described the process of adjustment in terms of an organizational decision process, which is viewed as a series of conscious or unconscious activities terminating in a choice among alternatives. The strategies for dealing with the environment are basically competitive or cooperative, and the subtypes of cooperation are bargaining, cooptation, and coalition. These forms can be ordered according to the degree of environmental control they provide over group goal-setting decisions.

The religious organization is often caught in competitive interaction with its environment. This may affect the sphere of specifically religious activities (preaching, retreats and missions, promoting religious organizations, and so forth) when the interests of two or more religious groups conflict. Or it may involve nonreligious activities in which the group is apostolically engaged. Religious groups involved in modern education are *ipso facto* caught up in the intense, though subtle, competition flourishing in modern education. Competition partially controls the group's choice of goals by forestalling arbitrary choices and by weeding out groups that provide services the environment is not willing to accept. Competition also forces on the group a certain standard of efficient operation that is essential if the group is to survive.

Bargaining is defined by Thompson and McEwen as "the negotiation of an agreement for the exchange of goods or services between two or more organizations."[16]

---

[15] Thompson and McEwen, "Organizational Goals . . . ," *op. cit.*
[16] *Ibid.,* p. 26.

Every group must operate within a context of organizational relations that are not static. Bargaining provides an important means for reviewing these relationships and determining future patterns of activity satisfactory to other groups. To the extent that other organizations are essential to the functioning of the religious group, bargaining exercises an influence on the decision process of that group.

Cooptation is defined as "the process of absorbing new elements into the leadership or policy-determining structure of an organization as a means of averting threats to its stability or existence."[17] This is the type of change the Church faces in confronting the question of increased responsibility for the layman. The question has been answered in many ways by religious groups, such as permitting laymen to function as trustees of colleges, universities and hospitals, placing laymen in responsible positions of administration in various institutions, and so on. It has often been found that responsible participation in the work and policy formation of the religious group, particularly with regard to its apostolic functions, is a most effective way of gaining environmental support and cooperation.

The final form of cooperation is *coalition,* "the combination of two or more organizations for a common purpose."[18] Coalition is extremely rare among religious groups, but is found more often in institutions with which religious groups are associated. For example, coalition is common among educational institutions which carry on large-scale research or fund-raising

---

[17] *Ibid.,* p. 27.
[18] *Ibid.,* p. 28.

projects; a religious group operating such an educational institution thus can be indirectly involved in coalition.

Although environmental control exercises an influence on the group's goal-setting processes, it is not a one-sided influence. Not only does competition limit the goal-setting of the competitor, but also the competitor exercises an influence on the competing elements. Bargaining has an impact on all of the bargaining parties, as do competition and coalition. Goals, therefore, are the product of interaction among elements within the group and between the group and its environment. It can be said that the effectiveness of the group depends on the initiative exercised by those members of the group responsible for goal-setting. Also, to maintain itself an organization must give serious consideration to its goals and must take constant stock of its relations with the environment. Therefore, the group must possess effective mechanisms to keep itself informed about environmental changes and to evaluate them in the light of the group's purposes. This is certainly true of the religious group, and the importance of the mechanisms becomes ever greater as the size of the organization increases and, correspondingly, as the final authority is removed even further from environmental contact.

The strategies for dealing with the environment, competition and cooperation, are also methods for gaining environmental support, but they differ in the "cost" to the group (coalition is more costly than bargaining in that more is surrendered to gain environmental support). Adopting the wrong strategy in a given situation may hinder the group in realizing its goals. It should be obvious, then, that it is essential to the religious group that superiors keep in constant contact with their members. And it is equally essential that superiors have an adequate picture of the pertinent changes in the environment, whereby they can estimate the effectiveness of the group's environmental interaction.

Most religious groups have mechanisms to facilitate communication; these include certain formally required practices such as voluntary manifestation of conscience, letters and reports to the higher superior, and visitations. But it is not only vitally important that there be higher forms of communication by which information may be channelled to the goal-setting member or members; these forms of communication must be used effectively to transmit information. This leads us to two further considerations: the necessity of feedback for the effective functioning of the group and the role of communication in the group process. We can postpone our consideration of communication for the present, but the problem of feedback is immediately relevant to the goal-setting decision process.

The concept of feedback was originally developed in the analysis of cybernetic mechanisms[19] concerned with regulation and control of operations in machines and animals. The concept has been extended to the analysis of social systems[20] and seems to be helpful in understanding certain group processes. In reference to the

---

[19] N. Wiener, *Cybernetics* (New York: Wiley, 1948).

[20] P. Nokes, "Feedback as an Explanatory Device in the Study of Certain Interpersonal and Institutional Processes," *Human Relations,* XIV (1961), 381-87. See also M. W. Pryer and B. M. Bass, "Some Effects of Feedback on Behavior in Groups," *Sociometry,* XXII (1959), 56-63.

group, feedback may be understood as information about the results of group operations. Feedback is essential to the attainment of group goals; if it is inadequate or is ignored, the results will be ineffective operation, failure, and possibly disintegration of the group.

In applying the concept to social processes, Nokes has suggested a relationship between anxiety and autistic (self-absorbed) thinking, on the one hand, and the neglect of feedback in group processes on the other; neglect of feedback, it is suggested, may produce a condition of imperfect contact with reality (always undesirable) that can be pathological. The basic problem, for an individual or for a group, is one of adjusting to reality. One cannot simply prescind from reality; one must either control it or be controlled by it. To deal effectively with the environment, accurate information must be obtained about what is taking place in it. The classic example of the catastrophic effects that can result when feedback is neglected is Adolf Hitler, who seems to have lived in a fantasy world, refusing to listen to reports of destruction from Allied bombings and, at the end, signing orders for attacks by armies that existed only in his mind.

To neglect feedback is a common temptation, and it can have especially harmful effects when it infects those who hold positions of authority. The more primary the relations within the group (the more face-to-face they are), the more easily is feedback communication maintained. This is certainly true in religious groups, especially in smaller communities. There is a twofold danger, however. On the one hand, members may tend to isolate the superior and fail to keep him informed about what is happening in the community;

this may result from fear that the superior will use such information against the interests of one or another member of the community, or it may be a manifestation of misconceptions about what the relationship between superior and member of the religious group should be.

On the other hand, there is a tendency in any authoritarian structure for the figure possessing power to seek security by relying more on the prestige of that power than by close interaction with the rest of the group. Administration is always difficult, and it is made more difficult by a continual inflow of information from the environment. The information is never quite what one would wish it to be, and it has an unhappy habit of creating one problem after another. Unless the superior has the maturity and self-possession to live and work in the flux of real problems, he can be tempted to seek the more peaceful atmosphere of an arbitrary administrative orientation and thereby neglect feedback. Such neglect can be the cause of anxiety in the member and of autistic thinking in the superior. And when the superior wants feedback information but his subjects won't communicate, this can be a source of anxiety for him.

It is important, therefore, that we gain some understanding of the communication process within the group. When we realize that social processes are based on interactions among individuals and that interaction requires some kind of communication, verbal or otherwise, among the interacting agents, we can appreciate the fact that communication theory embraces practically the whole of group life. There are a number of excellent approaches to the problem of communication, but we shall follow the synthesis provided by Newcomb,[21] who divides the process of social interaction into the following subprocesses:

1. Both cognitive and emotional dispositions (attitudes) are required toward other persons in the group and toward objects about which one can communicate.

2. At the same time, beliefs are acquired about the attitudes of others toward these same objects of communication.

3. These attitudes and beliefs about the attitudes of others toward given objects come to function interdependently as a system that has equilibrium properties.

4. Communication is initiated among individuals under conditions of disequilibrium in the system.

5. Following a communicative exchange, the equilibrium in the system tends to be restored.

6. The new state of equilibrium persists until it is disturbed by the receipt of new information, which is followed by a new disequilibrium-initiating communication.

Disequilibrium in the system is accompanied by a condition of "strain" or psychological tension that derives either from a perceived discrepancy between one's own attitude and the attitude of another or from uncertainty as to the other's attitudes. The amount of strain will depend on the degree of discrepancy perceived, the degree of attraction or rejection between oneself and the other person, the importance of the object of communication, the degree of one's certainty

---

[21] T. M. Newcomb, "Individual Systems of Orientation," in Koch, *op. cit.*, pp. 384-422.

about his own attitudes, as well as the degree of joint dependence of both persons on what is communicated as seen by the one communicating.

Working within this framework, Newcomb sets up a series of postulates from which the hypotheses are drawn. We can restate them as follows:

1. Certain combinations of attitudes toward an object of communication and the other person, together with that other person's perceived attitudes toward the same object, introduce strain into the system. The clearest instance is the combination of positive attraction to another person whose attitude toward the object is clearly at variance with one's own.

a. If the attraction involves respect for the other's knowledge about the object, one's own divergent attitude may be in error. This would involve a state of tension in which the threat of error would prompt one to communicate about the object and thus reduce the perceived discrepancy. This would be true of a religious subject who, while disagreeing with certain administrative practices of his superior, at the same time realizes that the superior is in a position to know more about the relevant conditions than he is.

b. If the attraction involves trust in the other's willingness to be helpful, cognitive discrepancy can interfere with the communication through which help may be given and received. The greater the trust, the greater the strain of discrepancy. In other words, the greater one's confidence in the other person's ability and willingness to help and the greater the need of such help, the greater the threat posed by the perceived discrepancy. This might be the condition of a religious who needs help with some personal problem and who knows that the superior would be most generous in trying to help, but who at the same time knows that the superior's attitudes toward the particular kind of situation are quite different from his own. Let us say that a religious teaching in a school needs certain facilities to improve the caliber of teaching, but the superior is opposed to such improvements and, instead, is in favor of raising the salaries of the lay faculty. If the superior is trusted and respected, communication would be the preferred means of reducing the tension.

c. If positive attraction involves personal attraction, a discrepancy of attitude might threaten the relationship, either by overt conflict or the threat of rejection. The greater the liking, the greater will be one's certainty, and the greater the perceived certainty of the other, the greater will be the strain. This would not usually be a factor in the superior-member relationship, but it would come into play very frequently in other parts of the group system.

d. Under any condition of positive attraction, uncertainty as to whether discrepancy exists can produce tension or threat. Often, the reluctance of the religious superior to communicate with his members about many of his attitudes can serve as the source of uncertainty and subsequent threat. This is particularly true of matters affecting the individual member personally — assignments, status changes, and so on.

The conditions that induce strain are usually the same when attraction is negative as when it is positive. Newcomb, however, distinguishes the orientation to the same object *because of* negative attraction to the other from the orientation that occurs *in spite of* negative attraction to the other. In the former it is the perceived threat from the other that prompts an orientation toward objects related to the threat; consequently, the greater the threat, the greater the strain. In the latter instance, however, our attention may be directed to the object for some reason independent of our negative attraction to the other, so there is no reason to suppose that strain will increase with negative attraction. It is more likely to increase with the importance of the object. Thus, if a member has some reason to fear or distrust his superior, he will endeavor to find out what actions the superior intends to take that may affect himself; his orientation to these actions comes about because of his negative attraction to the superior, and communication will occur either directly with the superior or indirectly through another informed party. If the same member is interested in something that is not connected with a threat from the superior, we would have no reason to expect communication in this regard.

2. The instigation to communicate is a learned response to such strain on the part of socialized human beings. The probability of communication depends on the strength of the instigation, the occurrence of situations that permit communication, and the strength of the forces that oppose communication. Communication is not the only means of relieving situational strain, but it is one that civilized men have learned to use because of its effectiveness in reducing threat. Instigations to

communicate take the following forms of system strain:

a. The other person is perceived as possessing information that the self lacks and wants, or, conversely, the other is perceived as lacking some information the self possesses.

b. The self wishes to confirm a tentative observation or hypothesis.

c. The other is seen as devaluing an object that the self values, or vice versa. In this instance, the communication will usually take the form of persuasion.

d. Uncertainty regarding emotional discrepancy may instigate communication in the form of inquiry or assertion in order to reduce the uncertainty.

3. Following communication, changes occur in the system of orientation so that strain is reduced. The probability of reduction in strain depends on the intensity of attraction to the other person, the degree of perceived discrepancy, the amount of competing attraction to other persons and/or groups, and so forth. The sort of positive attraction found in respect and trust is required for reduction of strain, particularly when it is a question of transmitting information. When emotional discrepancy is observed, a communicative exchange can often increase the discrepancy and, therefore, increase the strain.

It would seem, then, that the same condition of respect and trust would be required in this instance and that other conditions, such as the degree to which the person is committed to his present attitude, must be similarly harmonized. The stronger one's commitment to a present attitude, the less likely it is that communication would lead to a change of that attitude and a consequent reduction of strain. Since communication is a learned response, the failure of communication to reduce strain and tension may be expected to decrease the probability of fruitful communication. It is important for the group process, therefore, that the limiting conditions for effective communication be maintained as far as possible. Unless a superior maintains an atmosphere of mutual respect and trust in his dealings with his community, he can expect communication and the essential element of feedback to suffer.

4. Under certain conditions, changes can occur that will reduce strain without any open communication. As we have seen, strain depends on several variables (attraction, perceived discrepancy, and so forth) that can change in two general ways: by receipt of information (through direct experience or communication) or by certain autistic, or self-centered, operations on previously received information. Such operations may take the form of memory loss, rationalization, or cognitive distortions of one kind or another. Changes brought about by receipt of information and by autistic operations are both adaptive; the receipt of information tends to help the group adapt to its environment (environmental feedback), whereas autistic changes tend to serve the primary purpose of reducing strain within the group.

Consequently, the group can either supplement the receipt of information or substitute for it. The latter will most often occur under conditions that impede communication, such as absence of opportunity for communication and negative attraction. The supplementary function will come into play more often when the immediate effects of communication are to increase or induce strain. The situation we have already discussed, in which a superior neglects feedback, can also be regarded as a sort of autistic substitution for communication, motivated by the need to reduce strain in the system. However, such substitution runs the risk of exposing the group to environmental maladaptation.

5. Relations of interdependence within the systems of orientation make it possible for alternative changes to produce equivalent effects on strain. Newcomb points out that strain varies as a function of several variables, and, hypothetically, strain reduction can occur under a number of conditions: (a) reduction of strength of attraction; (b) reduction of object relevance; (c) reduction of *perceived* object relevance (to the other person); (d) reduction of importance of communication about the object; (e) reduction of *perceived* importance of the object to the other person; (f) changes in emotional or cognitive structure of one's attitudes so that they become more similar to the perceived attitudes of others; (g) changes in the *perceived* attitudes of others.

Such patterns of interaction do not take place in a vacuum. They are the product of forces operating within the group. Festinger[22] has attempted to define some of these forces that operate within a group to bring about communication. In the system of orientation involving a communicator, a co-communicator, and an object of communication, we have seen some of the elements involved in interpersonal communication as

22 L. Festinger, "Informal Social Communication," *Psychological Review*, LVII (1950), 271-82.

related to reduction of strain. There are forces at work within the group, as a group, that determine the patterns of communication. Festinger designates pressure toward uniformity as one of the major forces determining communication.

Two important sources of pressure toward uniformity are social reality and group locomotion. The first of these may be defined as the opinions, attitudes, and beliefs present in a group. Its importance was stated succinctly in the famous theorem of W. I. Thomas: If men define situations as real, they are real in their consequences. Human beings respond not only to the objective dimensions of a situation but also to the meaning they have assigned to it. Social reality is, therefore, opposed to physical reality. For example, if the question is raised whether it is snowing outside or not, the answer will depend primarily on sensory evidence; in this instance dependence on physical reality is high and dependence on social reality is low. If it is plain to me that snow is falling, my opinion will not rely on the opinions of others.

If, however, the question deals with matters that cannot be determined from the inspection of physical reality, as whether President Eisenhower was or was not a great president, my own opinion in the matter will depend to a much greater extent on the climate of opinion in the group. Consequently, when dependence on physical reality is low, dependence on social reality tends to be high. The second important source of pressure toward uniformity is group locomotion. Group locomotion exerts pressures toward uniformity when such uniformity is required for the group to move toward its goal. Pressures will be greater, then, when members see that uniformity will facilitate group movement and, likewise, when members are dependent on the group for the attainment of their goals.

With this basic postulate, Festinger[23] sets up a series of hypothesis that are supported in varying degrees by experimental evidence. As in Newcomb's formulation, communications arising from group pressures are seen as instrumental, that is, as means for reducing the perceived discrepancy between communicators:

1. "The pressure on members to communicate to others in the group concerning 'item x' increases with increase in the perceived discrepancy in opinion concerning 'item x' among members of the group." Divergence of opinion increases the probability of communication. Lack of divergence is frequently a difficulty in religious groups where backgrounds and attitudes tend to be homogeneous. This is often reinforced by a common training in religious doctrine and practice.

2. "The pressure on a member to communicate to others in the group concerning 'item x' increases with increase in the degree of relevance of 'item x' to the functioning of the group." On this basis, religious would be expected to communicate more readily on matters involved in the spiritual and apostolic functioning of the community. Experience tends to bear this out, since problems related to the objectives and functioning of the group are recurrent and frequent topics in recreation rooms.

3. "The pressures on members to communicate to others in the group concerning 'item x' increases with increase in the cohesiveness of the group." Cohesive-

---

[23] *Ibid.*

ness, which will be taken up in a later section, deserves notice here in its relationship to the communication process. Cohesiveness is the resultant of all the forces that act on the members to keep them in the group. When attraction to the group is high, there is, presumably, a greater tendency for the member to become more engaged in the group process. In the religious group, therefore, the tendency for communication among the members to occur readily will depend to a certain extent upon the degree of cohesiveness in the group.

4. "The force to communicate about 'item x' to a particular member of the group will increase as the discrepancy in opinion between that member and the communicator increases." This merely particularizes the first hypothesis insofar as communication will occur in the direction in which discrepancy is seen to be greatest.

5. "The force to communicate about 'item x' to a particular person will decrease to the extent that he is perceived as not a member of the group or to the extent that he is not wanted as a member of the group." What is in question here is the *psychological group*, which can exist within the religious group. Forces within the community to break down cliques, as well as the requirements of charity, work directly against such subgroupings. But sometimes the forms of in-group can be quite subtle, with the result that communication with rejected members is impaired. If the rejected member happens to be the superior, this can also cause difficulties in government.

6. "The force to communicate 'item x' to a particular member will increase the more it is seen that communication will change that member's opinion in the desired direction." This is important in the superior-member relationship, for unless the superior maintains a position of flexibility and open-mindedness, or at least presents to his community an impression of willingness to listen and perhaps be persuaded, the lines of communication will tend to close.

7. "The amount of change in opinion resulting from receiving a communication will increase as the pressure toward uniformity in the group increases." Pressures toward uniformity not only increase the attempts to change opinion in others, but also produce a greater disposition to change in the members of the group. Just as discrepancy of opinion is muted in the religious group by similarity of training and background, so the strength of pressures toward uniformity is diminished by the uniformity of opinion that already exists and which creates a more or less homogeneous social reality in the group. On the other hand, the goals of the religious group are so highly valued and so central in the life of the group that a great deal of pressure toward uniformity can arise from this source. Consequently, although the community of social reality is a strong binding force in the group, it cannot be regarded as a strong force in communication. As we shall see later, this would be less true in the early stages of religious formation when social reality tends to be less homogeneous.

8. "The amount of change in opinion resulting from receiving a communication will increase as the strength

of the resultant force to remain in the group increases for the recipient." The attractiveness of the group for a member gives the group power over him to produce real change in his opinions and attitudes. This has great relevance for the formation process, but it also remains operative in later stages of the group process. It is possible for a religious to withdraw from the psychological group within the community and at the same time retain his allegiance to the religious group itself. He thus isolates himself from the influence of the psychological group yet remains under the influence of pressures from the religious group, conceived either as the local community or as the larger organization.

9. "The amount of change in opinion resulting from receiving a communication concerning 'item x' will decrease with increase in the degree to which the opinions and attitudes involved are anchored in other group memberships or serve important need-satisfying functions for the person." This hypothesis can be verified to a certain extent in the situation of increasing numbers of religious who have been drawn into intellectual and scholarly pursuits.

The problem has presented itself with peculiar intensity for religious who are put to the task of studying and working in scientific areas. The commitment to scientific pursuits carries with it attitudes and opinions that are part of a professional orientation and are rooted in membership in the scientific community, professional organizations, and so on. This orientation may create—and, in fact, often has created—tensions with traditional attitudes regarding the polarities of contemplation-apostolicity, obedience-initiative, and the like. Pressures toward uniformity in the religious group have been diminished, not only because of differences within the social reality of the group itself, but also because the effectiveness of such pressures is diminished by involvement of members in scientific groups.

10. "The tendency to change the composition of the psychological group (pushing members out of the group) increases as the perceived discrepancy in opinion increases." Uniformity of the in-group is thus purchased at the expense of the deviate. However, the extent to which this mechanism operates depends on other factors, such as importance of the deviate to the functioning of the group, attraction between himself and other members, the degree to which communication is perceived as possible, and so forth. If the individual possesses a high degree of power or attraction and if the lines of communication are kept open, he is less likely to be excluded from the psychological group. But if these factors are lacking, the alternative to reduction of strain is a self-centered, or autistic, mode of functioning that is at once detrimental to the group life and devastating to the individual.

11. "When conformity exists, the tendency to change the composition of the psychological group increases as the cohesiveness of the group increases and as the relevance of the issue to the group increases." The relevance of the issue would depend on the connection between the issue and the group's goals. Any factors that increase the force to communicate will also increase the tendency to reject persons who disagree with a particular opinion. In the religious community uniformity of opinion is expected and maintained regarding the

major orientation and goals of the group. The pressures toward uniformity in this regard are strong, and rightly so, since uniformity at this level is essential to the functioning of the religious group. As a result, uniformity can invariably be found in regard to objectives of the spiritual life, the fundamentals of the particular institute, and major objectives and goals of the organization.

But there is also a large area of possible discrepancy of opinion—in the matter of particular means, minor goals and objectives, and the like. It is in this realm of discrepant opinions and attitudes that possible divisive forces can come into play. If discrepancy of opinion is found in a group climate dominated by attraction to the group and by positive attraction among the members, it becomes a positive factor in the group process since it is a basic condition of communication. If, however, it is found in a group climate in which attraction to the group is lacking or in which the members are negatively attracted to each other, discrepancy becomes the mother of division. From this viewpoint, the importance of the requirements of religious charity can be easily appreciated, since not only is charity a basic requirement for personal sanctity and harmonious living, but also it is essential to the vital processes that enable the community to function and achieve its goals as a group.

3

Solidarity and Group Participation in the Religious Community

We have already seen the importance of cohesiveness in facilitating communication within the group. Cohesiveness within the religious community is of the greatest importance in effectively moving the group toward its professed goals. The present task is to attain a more adequate notion of cohesiveness, determining the factors that foster attraction to the group, as well as the effects cohesiveness produces in the group process.

Essentially, the reasons why a particular group attracts can be summed up in a twofold way: the group itself is the object of a need, and membership in the group is a means for satisfying needs outside of the group.[1] The religious often joins the religious group because he values the objectives of the group highly, and, consequently, the group is attractive because its goal is attractive. The religious' continued attraction to the group, however, resides not only in the continued

---

[1] D. Cartwright and A. Zander, "Group Cohesiveness: Introduction," in Cartwright and Zander, eds., *Group Dynamics* (Evanston, Ill.: Row, Peterson, 1953), pp. 69-94.

attractiveness of the goal but also in his perception that his group is effectively achieving that goal. If the member comes to believe that inefficiency, poor leadership, lack of resources, interpersonal tensions, and so forth are impairing the group's effectiveness, his attraction to it will be proportionately diminished. In general, when the group's goals are its primary source of attraction, the attracting force, or "valence," is an indicator of the strength of the goals' attractiveness and also of the probability that the group will reach its goals.

Attractive force can be increased by helping each member or potential member to understand more clearly that his personal needs can be satisfied by membership in the group. Given the normal human needs for self-fulfillment, the greater the prestige the member of the group possesses or perceives it is possible to possess, the more strongly he is attracted to the group. By no means a simple variable in the group process, prestige or status can be achieved in more than one line; in the religious group a few obvious indicators of prestige are authority, intelligence, expertness in a field valued by the group, and strength of character perceived in relation to ideals of personal perfection. To gain or maintain status can serve as a powerful motivation to conformity to group norms.[2]

An experiment of Berkowitz and Macaulay[3] on four- and five-man groups of college freshmen suggests that members who see themselves approximating but not

[2] O. J. Harvey and C. Consalvi, "Status and Conformity to Pressures in Informal Groups," *Journal of Abnormal and Social Psychology*," LX (1960), 182-87.

[3] L. Berkowitz and J. R. Macaulay, "Some Effects of Differences in Status Level and Status Stability," *Human Relations*, XIV (1961), 135-48.

achieving their goal of secure high acceptance in the group tend to become strongly attracted to it. The conditions of the experiment made a possible change in status a variable. The results showed that high-status members whose status could change were more highly attracted to fellow members—both as social and as work partners—than those whose status was more stable. It has also been shown experimentally that members who were made to feel accepted found the group more attractive than those who were made to feel poorly accepted.[4] The effect of high or low acceptance was observed to be much stronger in persons with low self-esteem than in those with high self-esteem. Members with lower self-esteem evidently have a stronger need for acceptance from others.

In line with this last point, some authors have emphasized the group's protective function, in that it may serve to protect from threat or to satisfy a need for security. The cohesiveness of bomber crews was considerably heightened, for example, when crew members became aware that each was dependent on the others for his personal security.[5] Similarly, Schachter's results seem to indicate a positive relation between anxiety and the tendency to participate in groups that reduce the anxiety level.[6] Protective motivation may often be influential as an attraction to a religious group, and the religious group must have means to protect itself from

---

[4] J. Dittes, "Attractiveness of Group as a Function of Self-Esteem and Acceptance by Groups," *Journal of Abnormal and Social Psychology*, LIX (1959), 77-82.

[5] R. Grinker and S. Spiegel, *Men Under Stress* (Philadelphia: Blakiston, 1945).

[6] S. Schachter, *The Psychology of Affiliation* (Stanford, Calif.: Stanford University Press, 1959).

this possibility. Unfortunately, awareness of this motivation has not always been perceived.

Father Moore's statistics on the frequency of schizophrenia among female religious prompted the conclusion that religious life, particularly that of cloistered contemplative orders, attracted pre-schizoid types to the religious group.[7] The properties of religious life, such as silence, that tend to emphasize withdrawal from the world, intermesh very neatly with the pre-schizoid's needs to reduce anxiety levels by isolation and withdrawal. It may also occur on less pathological levels where the security and orderliness of religious life would, by reducing anxiety, reinforce attraction to the group.

The religious group constitutes a stratified or differentiated social system within which different classes of members are able to find varied kinds of gratification. What would satisfy the needs of some would not satisfy the needs of others. The members of the religious group who have highly specialized roles are apt to regard their membership more as a means than an end in itself. On the other hand, members who do not have any special responsibilities tend to view membership itself as an end.[8] Specialization is a common aspect of religious group life, particularly when apostolic activities demand specialized professional training. The distinction be-

---

[7] T. V. Moore, "Insanity in Priests and Religious," *American Ecclesiastical Review*," XCV (1936), 485-98, 601-13. See also Sister M. William, "Maladies mentales des religeuses," *Supplement de la Vie Spirituelle*, XII (1959), 295-305, as well as "The Incidence of Hospitalized Mental Illness among Religious Sisters in the United States," *American Journal of Psychiatry*, CXV (1958), 72-75.

[8] J. Tsouderos, "Organizational Change in Terms of a Series of Selected Variables," *American Sociological Review*, XX (1955), 207-10.

tween professionals and nonprofessionals creates a prestige system within the group from which the nonprofessionals do not benefit. Nonprofessionals, however, can
receive other benefits derived from outside the professional system.[9] In any one dimension or any combination of several dimensions, a member can achieve a
position of higher valuation within the group, as well
as a resulting increase in the strength of attraction to
the group.

Attraction to the group has concomitants and consequences that profoundly affect the individual's participation in its life. The more strongly a particular member is attracted to the group, the greater value he will
usually attach to group goals,[10] the more closely he will
adhere to group standards of behavior, and the more
ready he will be to protect those standards by exerting
pressures on or rejecting persons who transgress them.[11]
Such members are also less likely to show nervous symp-
toms and more apt to find security or release from tension in membership activities.[12] On the interpersonal
level, Zander and Havelin[13] have also discovered that
persons are attracted to other members whose competence is closest to their own and that attraction to the
group increases as the group's competence increases.

The individual, in fact, often finds himself psychologically drawn into activities and toward or away from

[9] J. M. Jackson, "Reference Group Processes in a Formal Organization," *Sociometry*, XXII (1959), 307-27.
[10] A. Zander and A. Havelin, "Social Comparison and Interpersonal
Attraction," *Human Relations*, XIII (1960), 21-32.
[11] Schachter, *op. cit.*
[12] S. Seashore, *Group Cohesiveness in the Industrial Work Group*
(Ann Arbor, Mich.: Institute of Social Research, 1954).
[13] Zander and Havelin, "Social Comparison . . . ," *op. cit.*

goals by the action of the group. Horwitz,[14] in studying the effects of group participation in motivating members to complete group tasks, has discovered that tension can be aroused for goals that the individual holds for the group. Just as with purely personal goals, the tension is reduced when the group completes the task and is not reduced when the task is interrupted. The attitude a member may have toward disagreements between his own decisions and those of the group has definite influence on the arousal and reduction of tension.

When the individual wants to complete the task and the group decides not to complete it, the individual's path to the goal is blocked. When the individual does not want to complete the task and the group decides to complete it, the individual is borne along toward that which he wishes to avoid. The level of tension is higher in the latter circumstance, in which the individual is coerced by the group, than in the former situation, in which he is frustrated. It was also found that tensions encouraging agreement with other members of the group exist alongside tensions generated by the group task, and that frequent dissent from the group decision will leave these tensions unreduced. In the more deviant members of the group, tensions involved in agreement tend to supplant tensions involved in the task.

The motivation underlying the individual's choice of a goal for the group does not differ, basically, from the motivation underlying his choice of goals for himself. The choice depends on the valuation he places on the

14 M. Horwitz, "The Recall of Interrupted Group Tasks: An Experimental Study of Individual Motivation in Relation to Group Goals," in Cartwright and Zander, *op. cit.*, pp. 370-94.

reward he will obtain for attaining the goals, on the effort required to reach the goal, and on the probability that the goal can be attained by himself or the group. The influences affecting the individual while in the process of forming certain preferences for group action stem from his personal motives as well as from his concern for the group's basic goals and its well-being in the social environment.

The interaction of these influences in determining the individual's evaluations is undoubtedly complex and certainly not well understood. A broad range of individual differences is common, inasmuch as personality factors and relationships between the individual and the group play such important roles in the process. Differences may arise from such factors as degrees of attraction to the group, degrees of acceptance by the group, position in the group, and so on.[15] For the member of a religious group, it is more a question of accepting already determined goals than of actively choosing them. There is, however, always room for adjusting the goals of the group according to its relationship with the social environment, and within this area of adjustment the individual religious can contribute to the formulation of goals—even though officially that function is part of the superior's office.

Many elements bear on the readiness with which a member accepts group goals. The assessment of the personal consequences of acceptance is an important factor; if the member believes that the group goals adequately reflect his personal motives, acceptance should be quick. The relative clarity of the group situation,

---

[15] D. Cartwright and A. Zander, "Individual Motives and Group Goals," in Cartwright and Zander, *op. cit.*, pp. 345-69.

that is, specific definition of the goal or of the proper procedures for attaining the goal, is also an important element. The clarity or obscurity of the group situation tends to be reflected in the individual members, not in terms of the objective group situation but in terms of the perception of that situation which the individual possesses. Unclarity may thus result from the group's objective unclarity about its goals and the means to attain them, or it may result from the individual's failure to understand the goals even when they are clear to the other members. The unclarity may also be a consequence of defective communication within the group. In any case, this lack of clarity affects the individual's adjustment in much the same way as confusion regarding individual goals would affect it. Similarly, the effect extends to the relationship between the individual and the group as such.

Under experimental conditions, Raven and Rietsma[16] have found that by varying the clarity of group goals and group paths toward these goals, the members of the group who clearly see and fully understand the group goal and group path manifest closer involvement with this goal, greater sympathy with group emotions, and a greater readiness to accept influence from the group. These members experience stronger feelings of belonging and are better equipped to perceive social differentiation in the group.

In the context of the religious group, it cannot be presumed that clarity about group goals and paths is always present. Under the careful surveillance of ecclesi-

---

16 B. H. Raven and J. Rietsma, "The Effects of Varied Clarity of Group Goal and Group Path upon the Individual and his Relation to his Group," *Human Relations*, X (1957), 29-44.

astical authorities, the formal documents that contain
the basic statement of group goals and objectives and
the paths to attain them are explicit and clear enough.[17]
But the contents of such documents must be communicated to the members; as a result, any breakdown in
communication will result in obscuring otherwise clearly stated norms. Furthermore, no written document can
be translated into vital activity without interpretation,
and interpretation demands further communication,
thus creating further problems of this nature. In addition to the formal documents of the religious organization, goals of local groups must be formulated and communicated clearly if objective conditions of clarity are
to prevail. Consequently, there is a considerable area
in which unclarity regarding specific goals and paths
may exert influence.

A certain amount of research has been devoted to
attempts to determine the relation between attraction
to the group and acceptance of group goals and the dimensions of the individual personality. There is evidence to support the hypothesis that when a person's
attitude toward the group is positive, he is more in-
clined to consider the group's goals as similar to those
he desires for the group and he will tend to perceive
accurately those group goals with which he agrees.
When his attitude toward the group is negative, the
tendency to perceive goals with which he does not
agree is not quite as strong.[18] Thus, the perception of

---

[17] Another relevant factor in the formulation of the religious group's
goals is that in many religious organizations the constitutions and
rules were written in a remote historical setting and in a cultural
context that was considerably different from contemporary culture.
[18] V. H. Vroom, "The Effects of Attitudes on Perception of Organizational Goals," *Human Relations*, XIII (1960), 229-40.

group goals and their relationship to personal goals depends to some extent on the perceiver's personality characteristics. If he has a positive attitude toward the group, he will usually attribute his own attitudes, opinions, and goals to the group; if his attitude is negative, he is apt to deny the same attitudes, opinions, and goals in the group.

But there is also some evidence to suggest that attitudes toward the group and attraction to certain goals are related to personality factors. It is a common observation that some people will cease striving and, perversely, even depreciate a goal when they are prevented from attaining it; others will increase their efforts when frustrated and give the appearance of valuing the goal even more highly under such conditions. Some lose all interest in the goal once they have attained it, whereas others continue to hold it in high esteem. Experimental indications suggest that such differences can be linked to variations in self-evaluation.[19] This argument contends that persons who evaluate themselves positively in regard to an ability considered necessary for goal achievement tend to value the goal highly when they achieve it and lowly when they don't. Persons who evaluate themselves negatively on the same ability will tend to devalue the goal when they obtain it and esteem it highly when they fail to obtain it. The results support these generalizations, but not unequivocally; this suggests that although the relationship is sufficiently valid, there may be other factors operating to complicate the picture.

---

[19] J. Israel, "The Effect of Positive and Negative Self-Evaluation on the Attractiveness of a Goal," *Human Relations*, XIII (1960), 33-47.

These indications can be reinforced somewhat by other similar findings. The positive relationship between group acceptance and attraction to the group was found to be stronger for members with low self-esteem; consequently, Dittes[20] suggests that low self-esteem can be taken as an index of strong need for acceptance by the group. Conversely, by varying the degree of unity in the group and its success or failure, it has been demonstrated that greater unity is positively related to a tendency for members to evaluate themselves in accord with the group success. Group failure produces tendencies that impair the conditions of group identification. The members of failing groups possessing high unity display less confidence in performing individual tasks than members of successful groups.[21] The temptation is strong to interpret these findings so as to claim that there is a positive relationship between group attraction, goal attraction, self-evaluation, and self-esteem. Although the relationship is plausible, the evidence is not strong enough to use as a basis for inferences about religious life. The positive relation between self-evaluation and goal attraction, for example, cannot be immediately extended to a generalization about personality, since high evaluation regarding a particular ability may or may not be related to general good self-regard.

However, other indications that we have mentioned make it clear that effective and rewarding participation in group activities demands a certain amount of personal security and individual maturity. It must be re-

---

[20] Dittes, "Attractiveness of Group . . . ," *op. cit.*
[21] A. Zander, B. Stotland, and D. Wolfe, "Unity of Group, Identification with Group, and Self-Esteem of Members," *Journal of Personality,* XXVIII (1960), 463-78.

membered that the group—and this is particularly true of the religious group—is a system of personal interaction. This interaction can be dominated by a realistic task-orientation, or it can be dominated by emotional interplay among the members. The former orientation is unquestionably to be preferred, and the extent to which it is realized will depend on the capacity of members to cooperate maturely, responsibly, and without undue emotional reaction in the activities of the group.[22] Consequently, the personal maturity of members contributes positively to the proper functioning of any group. In the religious group, where the total life situation is involved, tendencies to emotionality can exert a much greater than ordinary influence on the functioning of the group and on the personal adjustment of its members.

As long as a member receives satisfaction for needs and desires, he will want to maintain the status quo, either by keeping the group culture as it is or by working to ensure the group's effectiveness. It has been shown frequently that members who are highly attracted to a group act for its good more often than those who are less attracted.[23] Similarly, those who are highly

---

[22] In speaking of the dominance of task-orientation or of emotionality, we are referring to the predominant orientation that characterizes the group culture. This does not imply complete homogeneity in the activities of the group. Apostolic activity should achieve a balance of work and emotionality that is quite different from the balance achieved in healthy and enjoyable recreation. The former balance is weighted heavily toward the work orientation, the latter more toward the emotional orientation. But in neither situation should emotionality be permitted to dominate the interaction. The point is that the immature person allows the emotionality inherent in almost every human interaction to dominate.

[23] D. Cartwright and A. Zander, "Group Cohesiveness: Introduction," in Cartwright and Zander, *op. cit.*, p. 88.

attracted to a group more frequently assume group responsibilities,[24] more readily participate in meetings,[25]
show greater persistence in working toward difficult
goals,[26] attend group meetings more frequently, and
remain members longer.[27] They are also more ready to
try to influence other members of the group,[28] more
willing to listen to others, more receptive to others'
opinions, and they actually change their minds with respect to the opinions of others more often than less
attracted members.[29]

These findings have been demonstrated with experimental groups in more or less superficial contexts, such
as group discussions, but the consistency of the results
suggests that the principles may apply quite readily to
the more complex context of the religious group and
religious life. The strength of the attraction each religious has for the group plays an important part in the
degree to which he lives out his commitment to the religious life. On the group level this attraction is an essential element in providing the conditions under which
effective participation in group functions and the car-

[24] C. Larson, "Participation in Adult Groups" (doctoral dissertation,
University of Michigan, 1953).

[25] K. Back, "Influence Through Social Communication," *Journal of
Abnormal and Social Psychology*, XLVI (1951), 9-23.

[26] M. Horwitz, R. Exline, M. Goldman, and F. Lee, *Motivational
Effects of Alternative Decision Making Process in Groups* (Urbana,
Ill.: University of Illinois, College of Education, Bureau of Educa-
tional Research, 1953).

[27] P. Sagi, D. Olmstead, and F. Atelak, "Predicting Maintenance of
Membership in Small Groups," *Journal of Abnormal and Social Psychology*, LI (1955), 308-11.

[28] S. Schachter, "Deviation, Rejection and Communication," *Journal
of Abnormal and Social Psychology*, XLVI (1951), 190-207.

[29] Back, "Influence through Social Communication," *op. cit.*

rying on of such vital group processes as communication can be achieved.

The interaction process within the group maintains the structure of the social system by drawing highly valued members into the more central positions and forcing less valued members either into peripheral positions or rejecting them altogether. Within the religious group this may take any one of several subtle forms. Centrality can be associated with being made a superior, with being given some choice job that enjoys prestige, with social acceptance in the community (acceptance into the in-group of the community), or with assignment to certain preferred houses or tasks. The forces that shunt less valued members to the periphery of the group rarely cause total separation of a full-fledged member from the religious organization, but they very often do just that in the early stages of formation, before the less valued member has been able to identify with the group along other than prestige lines.

At later stages of the religious life, such pressures can have devastating effects on the devalued member. The group process acts in a way to deny him the satisfaction of his deepest personal needs, with the result that his strength of attraction to the group is diminished and his participation becomes marked by the negative correlates of low attraction. When interaction among members is operating most effectively, only members who in some way contribute to the group will ultimately remain in it. Such dynamic interaction implies that the system is constantly in a state of flux; some members are moving toward more central positions and others away from such positions. The impact of this process can be appreciated when we recall that the religious life, and therefore participation in the group process of the religious community, is a total engagement that embraces the whole man and all facets of his life. It is precisely a *state* of life and not merely a tangential membership. Therefore, if the group process tends to deny the individual essential gratifications, leaving the group is not so simple a matter as quitting one's job; the rejection affects one's whole life and not merely an isolated area of functioning.

In the process of social interaction, the individual tries to maximize personal gratification and minimize deprivation. The prestige system of the group generates certain evaluative signs that are transmitted in face-to-face contact, and the level of gratification the individual achieves is related to the kind of signs he receives from other members. Jackson[30] has extended this generalization to the following hypotheses:

1. In any group or organization a person's attraction to membership is directly related to the magnitude of his social worth.

2. The magnitude of the positive relationship hypothesized above varies directly with the volume of interaction the person has with other members of the group.

3. When alternative group orientations are possible for a person, his relative attraction to membership in one or another group is directly related to his relative social worth in the groups considered.

4. The magnitude of the positive relationship hypothesized varies directly with the volume of interaction the person has with other members of the groups under

---

30 Jackson, "Reference Group Processes . . . ," *op. cit.*

consideration. In other words, the strength of attraction to the group increases with an increase of esteem in the eyes of other members of the group and with the frequency of interaction with those members. It is important to remember, however, that no matter how valid the generalization may be, the conditions of interaction often change radically from one type of group to another.

Since the religious group is a unique type, such generalizations should be applied with caution. The process of social interaction within the religious community is conditioned by the factors regulating relationships among the members. Insistence on formality, for example, tends to reinforce a sense of dignity of the other person that sets a certain level of social valuation. Formality also has the effect of making social interaction uniform, so that discrepancies in social valuation are minimized. Even more significant, the role of charity, which is expected in the religious group, cannot be underestimated, since its effect may compensate for devaluative effects of the group process. It is well to note that charity does not always operate at its most effective intensity, but that the group process usually does.

It may be helpful to mention in passing the phenomenon of the "loner." Certain types of people prefer to avoid group participation whenever possible. Although they may be strongly attracted to the organization and work effectively for its goals, they prefer to work alone. Torrance[31] has suggested that the loner is afraid of the

[31] P. Torrance, F. Baker, K. De Young, S. Ghei, and J. Kincannon, *Explorations in Creative Thinking in Mental Hygiene: Alone or in Groups?* (Minneapolis, Minn.: University of Minnesota, Bureau of Educational Research, 1958).

group because he lacks a certain personal security and fears ridicule, rejection, or coercion from others. The loner can usually be absorbed within a large community, but in a smaller community continued isolation can make things difficult. However, the loner is not really an exception to the laws of group attraction; without some degree of social valuation there would be little to hold him in the group, although it is possible that sufficient gratification of other needs would keep him on the fringe.

Cohesiveness within groups also depends on the level of prestige of the group as compared with similar groups. If a group improves its position, the level of cohesiveness in the group also increases. Experimental subjects were more strongly attracted when they were told that their group's probability of successful achievement was higher than that of others,[32] and investigations of factors determining attractions to one group over others found that cohesiveness was greater in groups that performed at a superior level.[33] The general relationship between cohesiveness and attraction to the group is positive and reciprocal, in that the increase of attraction also increases cohesiveness and vice versa. However, the attraction of an individual member to a particular group is subject to extraneous influences. Some religious orders and congregations enjoy a higher level of prestige in the general culture than others, usually because there is a higher social value attached to

[32] M. Deutsch, "Some Factors Affecting Membership Motivation and Achievement Motivation," *Human Relations*, XII (1959), 81-95.
[33] E. Stotland, "Determinants of Attraction to Groups," *Journal of Social Psychology*, XLIX (1959), 71-80. See also L. Berkowitz, "Liking for the Group and the Perceived Merit of the Group's Behavior," *Journal of Abnormal and Social Psychology*, LIV (1957), 353-57.

the organization's goals and the group is effective in attaining them. This differential valuation will vary from culture to culture, but within a specific cultural context members may be more strongly attracted to one group than to others; the consequence of such cultural forces would be increased cohesiveness within the group.

In summary, attraction to the group depends on how well the group answers the needs of its members. The attractiveness of the group can be increased by making it meet those needs more effectively. Thus, a group will be more attractive the more it provides status and recognition, the more cooperative the relations among members, the freer the interaction, and the greater security it provides. The religious group scores fairly high on these counts. The religious vocation is accorded, at least in our culture and among Catholics, a high status value with respect to the overall culture; relations in the religious community, dominated and guided by charity, are more highly cooperative than in most other types of groups; and members of the religious group can be assured of a certain level of material security for the whole of their lives.

Experimental evidence indicates that a close relationship exists between group cohesiveness and the amount of mutual influence among members.[34] The reason is found in the fact that paralleling the degree to which members desire to remain in the group runs a tendency to originate and accept pressures calculated to preserve the group and move it toward its goals. Consequently, there is a direct relationship between

[34] L. Festinger, "Informal Social Communication," *Psychological Review*, LVII (1950), 271-82.

group cohesiveness and group power to bring about change in its members. Pepitone and Reichling[35] have reported an experiment in which members were attacked by an instigator both individually and collectively. Members sought to reduce this threat or retaliate against it, but their expressions of hostility were barred by certain internal, and perhaps external, restraints. The highly-cohesive group was able to manifest more hostility, to express it more directly, and to show less restrained physical behavior. These results were attributed to the highly cohesive group's ability to help members provide and accept support designed to overcome the restraints against removing the source of threat to the group or to its achievement of its goals.

Similar effects were found by Thomas,[36] who examined the interdependence among members created by a division of labor and cooperative effort to achieve team goals. Facilitation of efforts was achieved when members allowed others to perform their tasks successfully and strove toward group or individual goals in such a way that each member's efforts helped all others attain their respective goals. The results showed that the greater the facilitation among members in interdependent roles, the more frequently and strongly they experienced pressures to responsibility, speed of locomotion toward the goal, strain arising from working at the limits of ability and consequent fatigue, and finally group cohesiveness. Thus, facilitative interdependence may point a way in which group cohesiveness can be increased.

---

[35] A. Pepitone and G. Reichling, "Group Cohesiveness and the Expression of Hostility," *Human Relations,* VIII (1955), 327-37.
[36] B. J. Thomas, "Effects of Facilitative Role Interdependence on Group Functioning," *Human Relations,* X (1957), 347-66.

Central to the notion of facilitative interdependence is the sharing of responsibility in a way that every member feels he is contributing to the locomotion of the group toward its goals. Responsibility is often highly centralized in the religious community, with the result that the forces of attraction are diminished and effective functioning of the group is impaired. Although the effects can be damaging at any stage of religious life, they are especially harmful in the early stages, where the impact is felt not only in withdrawals from the group but also in defective formation in religious spirit and personal maturity. But we shall see more of this later.

Another area of experimentation has dealt with the relationship between group cohesiveness and productivity. There are two general approaches. The first suggests that the cohesive group is marked by good morale. Since the members like each other and get along well together, it should follow that increased cohesiveness is related to increased productivity. Unfortunately, experimental tests of this hypothesis have advanced some, but not sufficient, support for it.[37] The other approach suggests that cohesiveness is related to the attraction of the members for the group, so that an increase of cohesiveness is paralleled by the power of the group to influence its members. The power is equivalent to the magnitude of the force on the members to remain in the group.

Experimental evidence, however, indicates that there is no necessary relation between cohesiveness and high

---

[37]S. K. Bose, "Group Cohesiveness and Productivity," *Psychological Studies, Mysore,* III (1958), 20-28.

productivity. Highly cohesive groups are more likely to accept influences toward either higher or lower productivity, and often, as for example in the industrial slow-down,[38] the highly cohesive group responds in a negative fashion. In any case, it seems that the more cohesive group is better able to move toward its goals; higher productivity may not always be the goal to which it directs itself. When the influence of the group is brought to bear on members to increase productivity, both high and low cohesive subjects increase their output; but when the group influence is in the opposite direction, toward lowering productivity, it is the high cohesive subjects who respond to the group influence.[39]

Another area of research that has yielded significant results is the investigation of the effects of cooperation and competition among members on group functioning. Experimental indications seem to support the following hypotheses:[40]

1. In a cooperative situation individuals tend to perceive themselves as interdependent in such a way that the efforts of other members to attain the goal, and vice versa, are facilitated. In a competitive context, individuals perceive themselves as interdependent but also as each impeding goal attainment for the other.

2. There will be greater substitutability of actions

---

[38] J. Darley, N. Gross and W. Martin, "Studies of Group Behavior: Factors Associated with the Productivity of Groups," *Journal of Applied Psychology*, XXXVI (1952), 396-403.

[39] S. Schachter, N. Ellertson, D. McBride, and D. Gregory, "An Experimental Study of Cohesiveness and Productivity," *Human Relations*, IV (1951), 229-38.

[40] M. Deutsch, "The Effects of Co-operation and Competition upon Group Processes," in Cartwright and Zander, *op. cit.*, pp. 414-48.

directed to similar goals among cooperating individuals than among competing individuals.

3. In the cooperative situation positive emotional re-actions will be more frequent in response to the actions of others; negative emotional reactions will be more frequent in the competitive situation.

4. The power of the group to produce positive change will be greater among cooperating individuals than among competing individuals.

5. In the cooperative situation individuals will exhibit more helpfulness, whereas in the competitive situation they will exhibit more obstructiveness.

Individuals in the cooperative situation tended to manifest more of the following characteristics than did individuals in the competitive situation: coordination of efforts; diversity in the amount contributed by indi-vidual members; subdivision of activities; pressure toward achievement; attentiveness to fellow members; mutual comprehension of communications; common ap-praisals of comunications; orientation and orderliness; productivity per unit time; quality of production and discussion; friendliness during discussions; favorable evaluations of the group and its products; perception of favorable effects on fellow members; and incorpora-tion of the attitude of the "generalized other." No sig-nificant differences were found in amount of interest or involvement, in amount of specialization of function, or in the amount of learning.

It seems that not only is productivity increased by a cooperative orientation in the group, but also it has definite beneficial effects on the group process itself, particularly in small, face-to-face, primary groups.[41] The communication of ideas, coordination of efforts, friendliness, helpfulness, and pride in group membership, all of which are essential to the effectiveness of group operations, cannot be maintained when members are competing for mutually exclusive goals. Furthermore, as Deutsch points out, there is reason to believe that the competitive situation tends to produce greater personal insecurity through expectations of hostility from others.[42]

The importance of these findings for understanding the group process within a religious community cannot be overestimated. The life of charity that governs the group process in a religious group tends to eliminate the competitive motif, but it can be introduced in more subtle ways. This is particularly true in our American culture, where the theme of competition has come to dominate almost every facet of economic and social life. There are many situations in a religious community in which a spirit of competition can insert itself—sports, academic grades, fund-raising, currying favor with externs (especially students), running activities of one variety or another. But it is clearly a less desirable mode of operation, and, in addition, it has deleterious effects on community life.

[41] L. K. Hammond and M. Goldman, "Competition and Non-Competition and Its Relationship to Individual and Group Productivity," *Sociometry*, XXIV (1961), 46-60. See also A. J. Smith, E. H. Madden, and R. Sobol, "Productivity and Recall in Co-operative and Competitive Discussion Groups," *Journal of Psychology*, XLIII (1957), pp. 193-204.

[42] Deutsch, "The Effect of Co-operation . . . ," in Cartwright and Zander, *op. cit.*, pp. 414-48.

The cooperative situation involves a certain degree of mutuality, that is, not only must I choose to cooperate with someone else, but also he must choose to co-operate with me. Thus the choice to cooperate involves the two further factors of coordination and trust. The first implies that differences among the potential co-operators in perceptions of the cooperative path must be resolved. Trust implies that the person cooperating be trusting and the person with whom he cooperates be perceived as trustworthy. Basically, trust is a dimension of personality requiring that the individual have a certain degree of confidence in himself before he can begin either to have confidence in others or to present a face of trustworthiness to others.[43]

Deutsch[44] has been able to demonstrate experimentally that a cooperative orientation leads to highly predictable trusting and trustworthy behavior and, conversely, that a competitive orientation leads to suspicious and untrustworthy behavior. The relation also seems to be reciprocal, since it has been shown that trust increases the probability of cooperation and communication.[45] This is a very important finding, for it links the elements of cooperation, trust, and—in the light of our previous remarks on the relation between trust and communication—communication. A spirit of competition would be particularly harmful in the religious group in that it fosters mistrust and suspicion, which in turn tend to disrupt the essential process of communica-

---

[43] E. H. Erikson, *Identity and the Life Cycle* (New York: International Universities Press, 1959), pp. 55-65.

[44] M. Deutsch, "The Effect of Motivational Orientation upon Trust and Suspicion," *Human Relations,* XIII (1960), 123-39.

[45] J. L. Loomis, "Communication, the Development of Trust and Co-operative Behavior," *Human Relations,* XII (1959), 305-15.

tion. The maintenance of trust and trustworthiness, the capacity to cooperate in a way that the autonomy of the other person is respected and valued, and the ability to contribute responsibly to cooperative tasks are marks of a mature personality.

Since these functions are so central to the group process in religious life, the analysis of the group process throws into bold relief the necessity of having mature persons as members of the religious group. When the member assumes the role of superior, thus adding to his participation in the group the elements of power, prestige, and capacity to influence the group process, the necessity becomes very nearly absolute.

Besides the factors that tend to increase cohesiveness in the group, there are also factors that tend to decrease it and to lead to dissociation within and from the group. Often, when basic goals of the group are nonoperational, the group will tend to formulate operational subgoals that either support the goals of the group or do not. When such goals are not compatible with the over-all goals of the group, they can disrupt the functioning of the entire group. The whole process of splinter-group formation and the derivation of cliques has not received sufficient attention from social scientists, but these developments would seem to indicate some sort of breakdown in group process in which dissociation from the main body of the group occurs. Various factors can decrease the level of attraction to the group, as, for example, when members are expected to perform at a superior level.

Stotland[46] set up an experiment in which some subjects succeeded in an individual assignment that was

---

[46] Stotland, "Determinants of Attraction . . . ," *op. cit.*

done for the group, and others were made to fail. The
failures were naturally less attracted to the group. But
the significant finding was that when the group's expectations were low or the task important to the group,
decrease in attraction was greater than when group expectations were high or the task not important. Also,
the effect of failure on group attraction was confined
almost completely to persons with low self-esteem and
occurred hardly at all among persons with high self-
esteem.

Any kind of unpleasant experience in the group can
affect attraction to the group. In any group the member must assume responsibilities, for some of which he
does not feel adequately prepared. If his inadequacy is
a source of embarrassment, his personal attraction to
the group may suffer as a result. Consequently, the
group that makes excessive demands on its members
will be less attractive than one that operates more reasonably. More peripheral members can be pushed into
negative attitudes toward the group if they are required
to accept heavy responsibility or if they see that the
group is making disagreeable demands. In the religious
group, demands are often placed on members to fulfill
specific and responsible functions. Often, unforeseen
situations arise, vacancies are created by sickness or
death, new apostolic opportunities present themselves,
which create demands that must be met by the group.
In such circumstances, the prudent course would require that the member of the group best equipped to
fill the job be placed in the new position. This is not
always possible, so that the second best course would
be to choose a member whose attraction to the group
is sufficiently strong and whose maturity and self-

evaluation will motivate him to place a high value on the goal to which the group wishes to direct him.

The persuasion that has been current among religious organizations—that obedience requires perfect indifference to the demands of the group on individual members—can sometimes cloud the good judgment of superiors and lead them to make demands on members that plainly exceed their capacity or preparation. Regardless of the member's good disposition and honest effort, he cannot escape the dissociative effects of such excessive demands.

In summary, the force with which a person is attracted to the group is decreased when the needs that membership in the group satisfies are diminished or when the group itself becomes less suitable as a means for the satisfaction of existing needs. A member will be drawn away from the group when the net attractive force becomes negative rather than positive. Actual removal from the group will occur only when the sum of the forces driving him *away* from the group becomes greater than the sum of the forces attracting him *to* the group, plus whatever other restraining forces may be brought into play. This constellation of forces is always unique for each individual member of the group, insofar as the forces themselves operate through the perceptions of the individual, which in turn depend upon the special organization of the individual personality. But since personal adjustment is always the product of a continuing interaction between the individual and his environment—both physical and social (including, therefore, the group)—continued participation in the group or separation from the group is determined, at least in part, by forces stemming from the group process.

Defection from the religious life is one of the main problems that religious orders have to face. The problem is more acute in the early stages of religious life, when the younger religious are undergoing the period of trial and formation. Defections also occur at later stages of religious life, and when the defecting member is a priest or an older Sister or Brother, it can be tragic. The prototype of religious defection is the fallen-away priest. But in terms of the group process, defection and the mechanisms of defection are relevant not only to separation from the group but also to the kind of peripheral group participation that is marked by tepidity, sloth, the failure of religious ideals, lack of productivity, and so forth.

Separation from the group is a sufficiently frequent and serious problem, but the problem of peripheral participation is equally serious, if less dramatic. There are no reliable statistics on the frequency of the partial failures, the discontented members of religious groups, but there is no good reason to think that the percentage is any higher than in other professional groups. For those who live within the religious community, the problem assumes an added urgency: the motivational level of most religious is so high and such heavy demands are placed on them for various kinds of service that the luxury of the partial failure can be ill afforded.

More often than not, total or partial failure of the religious is interpreted as a breakdown in his spiritual life. His motivation slackens, he becomes tepid, he loses interest in spiritual things, such as prayer and meditation, he begins to neglect the rules, he manifests a spirit of pride and worldliness, and he soon sinks into a state of boredom with the whole routine of his religious life. In accounting for this sort of deterioration, the tendency is to ascribe the failure to the religious himself. This rationalization is not entirely wrong, and the fact that the religious is ultimately responsible, at least in part, for his own defection from his religious ideals has tended to throw other relevant factors into the background. The understanding of human behavior is never complete unless the total life situation has been brought into focus.

Our purpose in assembling this material on the group process is to suggest that such patterns of defection cannot be understood fully unless the interaction between the group and the individual is taken into account. Although placing the responsibility on the shoulders of the individual may help to relieve certain anxieties in other members of the group—particularly when superiors have been deeply involved in dealing with the defecting subject—this does not help to understand the process of defection. Nor does it foster the conditions in which intelligent action can be taken to remedy defects in the group's operation that may underlie the problem. Fichter[47] has called attention to the problem in the following terms:

> . . . it may be well to recall that Pope Pius XII asked for adaptation in religious organization not only that the apostolic work may be better performed, but also that the people performing it may be better adjusted. He asserted that some traditional customs—and this involves the matter of human relations and role per-

47 J. H. Fichter, S.J., *Religion as an Occupation* (Notre Dame, Ind.: University of Notre Dame Press, 1961), pp. 206-07.

formance—are no longer fitted either to the needs of the times or to the religious functionaries who are trying to answer these needs. This is another way of saying that the institutionalized structure in which functionaries work may require a certain amount of overhauling. The problem of the person who, after years of trying, still does not "fit in" the organization, may well be the problem of the organization's failure to adapt itself.[48]

One basic dimension of the problem is the tension between the bureaucratic and professional structures within the religious life.[49] Each structure bears within itself certain basic attitudes and values that determine conflicting courses of action. The bureaucratic structure places the emphasis on efficiency, conformity, obedience; it tends to require of members a certain degree of indifference and indeterminacy that makes them more ready to respond to superiors' directives. The professional structure stresses the contrary elements of professional competence and specialized training, initiative, personal responsibility, productivity, and so on. In its historic context, the bureaucratic structure was magnificently fitted to fulfill the needs of the organization.

In religious groups, where the works undertaken were sufficiently homogeneous to permit fairly ready interchange of individuals, along with reasonable expectation that the work would be done, the bureaucratic emphasis on administrative organization was a boon. The changing patterns of modern society have

---

[48] For Pius XII's remarks on religious life, see J. F. Gallen, "Pope Pius XII and the Religious Life," *Review for Religious*, XIV (1955), 3-11, 85-92, 123-38.

[49] Fichter, *op. cit.*, p. 208 *et passim*.

placed demands on the religious group that have forced it to modify its goals and diversify its activities, with the result that individual members must accept highly specialized functions that require extensive professional training and professional commitment.

If the religious group fails to commit itself whole-heartedly to such specialized apostolic tasks, with the result that the psychological in-group fails to value the contributions to the group process by specialized members, the specialized member can be forced into a more peripheral position and the forces of attraction to the group consequently lessened. When the attractive forces stemming from his participation in the nonreligious professional group are added to this rejecting force within the religious community, it is small wonder that the religious who is professionally trained does sometimes defect from the religious life. If, however, the attitudes of the religious community have become adaptable to the point where the position of the professional is properly esteemed in terms of the group's functioning and if the rewarding centrality to the group is allowed, the attractive forces on the professional will increase and the likelihood of defection thereby be diminished.

Specialization of function within the modern religious group is an important problem, primarily because the group process has failed to adapt properly somewhere along the line. The failure to adapt may stem from defective communication, insufficient feedback, excessive clinging to outmoded patterns of operation or values, and so on. The failure to adapt cannot help having devastating consequences for the effective operation of the group and its ability to attain its goals.

When the failure reaches this level, the functioning of the entire group is affected, with the inevitable result that cohesiveness is decreased and forces of attractiveness to the group are dissipated.

Adaptation is not merely a question of the modification in function of a few individuals or an isolated segment of the community. As long as the group is functioning as a group, that is, as long as the religious group exists, adaptation to some extent affects every member. If the individual, because of his personal insecurities or anxieties, fails to adapt with the group, the functioning of the group must suffer and the group has no recourse but to relieve the strain by redefining its boundaries and isolating that particular member. The group does not consciously and purposefully set out to exclude any of its members, which would be a rank violation of charity, but the group process will be set in motion without anyone in the group being responsible for it.

To the extent that an individual member is relatively unstable—dependent emotionally on the group or particular members of the group or participating in the group process in a manner somewhat less than mature—rejecting influences can have devastating effects on his functioning and adjustment. If we accept the description that Bion[50] has provided of the workings of emotionality within the group and if we add the further observation that interactions within the religious group so constitute the whole fabric of the religious' living situation that the religious life is preeminently a social

---

[50] W. R. Bion, *Experiences in Groups* (New York: Basic Books, 1961).

life,[51] it is difficult to avoid the conclusion that the defection, total or partial, of the individual religious is a symptom of the failure of the group process.

Our systematic knowledge of the patterns of emotional reactivity within the religious group is hardly sufficient at this time, but what we do know of emotional reactivity in other types of groups at least suggests that when we have pointed an accusing finger at the religious failure, we have not yet considered the full implications of his defection. If, however, we did not point the finger at him, we would be forced to look elsewhere to understand his failure. The latter can be a disturbing alternative.

---

[51] B. I. Mullahy, "Community Life," *Review for Religious,* XIV (1955), 141-50.

4

Religious Formation
and the Group

Religious formation is a process that is intended to transform the lay person who is drawn to the service of God in the religious life into a religious. The process is complex in that it aims at a transformation that affects the person's entire mode of existence. It is not simply a matter of training to fulfill certain apostolic functions; it also involves an inner transformation of attitudes, values, patterns of behavior, tendencies, and dispositions. Formation, therefore, aims at making the religious person a fully participating member of the religious group.[1]

Religious formation affects the core of the personality in a way that no other professional preparation attempts. The religious must be prepared not merely for a peripheral role function (the performance of some work or task that contributes to locomotion toward the group's goal), but for total engagement in a life situation that embraces, besides particular functions, a

---

[1] For a summary of documentation on religious formation, see J. F. Gallen, "Religious Clerical Formation and Sister Formation," *Review for Religious*, XIV (1955), 205-15.

framework for personal interaction in everyday activities. It is quite clear that personality factors and intrapsychic dynamics play a major role in contributing to or detracting from effective formation.

The psychodynamics of formation is a vast and complicated subject, which, despite its importance, we cannot take into consideration here. Our examination will be limited to the interaction between individual and group and to the role of the group process itself in religious formation. Even within these limits it will be possible to present only a fragmentary appraisal of the impact of group factors on the formation process, yet the attempt should bring to light important aspects of the adjustment process in religious life that have been consistently ignored or unrecognized in the past.

It is important to keep in mind the constructural picture of group interaction that we have already presented in detail (Chapter 2). The group constitutes a system of interaction surrounded by its environment and composed of individual agents. Each individual agent is considered as a complex of drives and dispositions that can be mobilized by interactions with other agents or with the total group system. The group's social system may be considered as exerting certain controls over interaction between persons and between the person and the environment through the medium of the group culture.

The culture of the religious group is quite stable and specific. Its stability is rooted in the fact that the goals and methods that the group adopts are governed by prescriptions of canon law, by the approved formulae of the institute, by the formal legislation of the organization, by a tradition of interpretation and application in accordance with the objectives of the organization and the "spirit" of the founder or foundress, and, usually, by an accretion of customs that regulate practical implementation. Its specificity derives from the nature of the group and from the particular apostolic objectives for which it exists. Thus, culture in a religious group is a more or less constant factor; any modifications are usually slight and gradual. From the point of view of formation, the problem is not so much one of mutual adaptation of individual and group as it is a problem of adapting the individual to the more or less stable values, attitudes, and patterns of behavior of the group.

We have seen that the capacity of the group to influence its members depends on the degree of cohesiveness in the group and on the strength of the forces on the member to remain in the group.[2] Cartwright has synthesized the major factors that characterize the group as a medium of change into several important principles.[3] The group's ability to influence its members depends upon the member's sense of belonging to the group, his attraction to it, the relevance of the issues to the basis of this attraction, the prestige of the influencing member or members, and the extent to which change is in conformity to group norms. Let us consider these factors in detail.

1. If the group is to be used effectively as a medium of change, those persons who are to be changed and

[2] S. Schachter, N. Ellertson, D. McBride, and D. Gregory, "An Experimental Study of Cohesiveness and Productivity," *Human Relations,* IV (1951), 229-31.

[3] D. Cartwright, "Achieving Change in People: Some Applications of Group Dynamics Theory," *Human Relations,* IV (1951), 381-92.

those who are to exert influence for change must have a strong sense of belonging to the same group.

The religious group, like any other permanent organization, has strong tendencies to foster in-group solidarity, which acts as a positive factor in preserving the group and helping it achieve its goals. One would expect it to be especially strong whenever the group process is so central to the need satisfaction and personal fulfillment of each of its members—as is the case in the religious group. Such strong in-group solidarity, however, tends to strengthen the force of rejection directed toward those not perceived as members of the group. The religious community can fall into a self-defeating situation, wherein it subtly rejects individuals from outside who are absolutely necessary to the preservation of the group. The conflict arises between what is felt, consciously or unconsciously, to be the psychological in-group and what is known to be the group as such. Speaking more technically, it is a conflict between the demands of the group as task-oriented and the demands of the group as governed by emotionality.

This tendency underlines the wisdom of separate houses of formation in religious orders, where the young religious are subjected to the in-group/out-group dynamisms to a lesser degree. In this context, too, they have the opportunity to grow in religious spirit and to develop a sense of identification with the group by achieving a rapprochement between their personal goals and needs and the goals and needs of the religious organization.

It is possible even in this setting for the in-group mechanism to operate, since even in these formative years the young religious are governed by superiors and subject to other established members of the group such as master or mistress of novices, teachers, mistress of juniors, and other officials. The contact of the young religious with the more mature religious in charge of them is extremely important. Not only is it possible but frequently it happens that a separation is effected between the young religious and their masters or mistresses. This can be brought about by various forms of preferment shown to the masters but not to the younger members, such as special places at table, and other privileges.

Such differences are to be expected, since the years of formation, especially the novitiate years, are intended as times for testing the young religious by depriving him of certain comforts and privileges and schooling him in the virtue he needs for living a mature religious life. These differences themselves are not important; what is important is the spirit with which they are implemented in the community. They can be implemented reasonably, since it is obvious that one cannot expect mature religious to live like novices. But they can also be implemented in a way that implicitly informs the younger members of the group that they do not really belong, that they are not really part of the community, that they are only more or less tolerated by it. Implicit in this communication is the threat, often consciously used by superiors and masters and mistresses of novices, that the younger member can be ejected if he steps out of line.

As consequences of this situation, the young religious' attraction to the group is decreased, group cohesiveness is damaged, the potential for significant identification with more mature members of the community is negated, and the power of the group to influence the younger member and effect in him or her the changes the community seeks is diminished.

2. The more attractive the group is to its members, the greater is the influence that the group can exert on its members.

We have already discussed this principle in the previous chapter. The question arises, however, as to *how* the attractiveness of the group can be increased for individual members. From a consideration of the influences we have seen exerting effects on group attractiveness, many means can be suggested. In general, the group will be more attractive when its prestige is higher than that of other groups. A particular religious group is constantly in competition with other professional groups and with other religious orders. Presumably, whatever can be done to enhance the prestige of the religious group as a way of life and a program of activity in comparison with other such vocations would increase the forces of attraction to the group. Also, the more the individual members are able to perceive the goals of the group as significant and valuable, the more attracted will they be to the group. This is nothing new, of course; spiritual writers have traditionally emphasized the dignity of the religious vocation and the nobility of the apostolic life.

What is particularly important to the process of formation is that attraction to the group for a particular young religious is directly related to the extent to which the group satisfies his particular needs. The roots of personal motivation are too complex to discuss, but the issue is so basic that repeated reflection on it does not begin to exhaust its ramifications. There are, nonetheless, in every religious certain basic human drives that are relevant to this issue.

Psychologists make a great deal of sexuality as a basic source of human motivation. Because it flies in the face of some of their most fundamental attitudes, the religious life, with its uncompromising demands for celibacy, is a phenomenon that confounds their understanding. In gross terms they would argue that the religious group not only cannot satisfy but even positively eliminates any satisfaction of a basic and universal human need—sex. Attraction to such a group, therefore, can be maintained only at tremendous cost in human potentiality. The presumption underlying this appraisal is shared by spiritual writers who evaluate the religious life as unnatural and entailing tremendous sacrifices.

One of the primary rationalizations for the rate of dropouts from religious groups is precisely that the lure of the flesh is too strong and the demands of celibacy more than weak human flesh can cope with. I do not find this orientation very persuasive, simply because it accepts uncritically too many basic presuppositions, most of which bear the strong imprint of cultural biases never subjected to rigorous scientific validation.

The argument is too complex and uncertain to develop here, but it seems likely that there are other basic human tendencies and dynamisms equal if not greater in importance than sex. To select only one, man has a powerful need to seek self-fulfillment and enrichment. I would tend to place this need for the individual to achieve a mature identity ahead of the lure of the flesh as a source of significant and nonpathological motivation. This is especially important in young religious of high school and early college ages, since this is precisely the period of their lives in which the identity crisis is most acute.[4]

If the young religious does not find himself growing into mature and responsible adulthood with a clear and secure sense of his identity as a person, as a man, as a religious, as a member of his particular religious group, the failure to realize his inner potentialities because of inhibiting group influences will decrease the group's attractiveness for him. Conclusive evidence is not available to support this hypothesis, but it is worth considering the possibility that rather than sexuality—the traditional scapegoat for defection from the religious group —a more significant area of failure for the religious is that of achieving personal maturity and identity. In the context of formation, the importance of the need for personal growth cannot be underestimated. The person who fails to achieve a mature identity often does find stability and a certain amount of false security in the religious group, and it is this very phenomenon that frequently accounts for the partial failure—the religious who fulfills neither the ideals of his religious profession nor the norms of personal maturity, yet who continues to live within the religious community.

3. In attempts to change attitudes, values, or behavior, the more relevant they are to the basis of attraction to the group, the greater will be the influence that the group can exert upon them.

This principle implies that the influence of the group over its members can vary, that it will be overwhelming in some areas and negligible in others. It is always difficult to discover what values or motives underlie the at-

---

[4] E. H. Erikson, *Identity and the Life Cycle* (New York: International Universities Press, 1959), pp. 88-94.

traction of an individual to a religious group, and it is correspondingly difficult to predict which areas of functioning in the individual will or will not be subject to strong group influence. It is not unreasonable to assume that primary motivations are usually related to spiritual values and concretely to the values embodied in the formally stated goals of the organization.

Superiors sometimes overlook the fact that what the members have dedicated themselves to is the organization in the fullness of its extent and in the most intelligent and functionally perfect form of its operation, not to a conception of the organization as projected by this or that superior, master of novices, mother general, or what have you. If the member has sufficient identity and maturity and sufficient awareness of the goals and values of the organization, he can perhaps bear with the imposed projection of a given superior, but this condition is not normal among young religious, particularly novices. Therefore, it is possible that in the early phase of his religious experience the young religious will find those values which he sought in the organization not being lived up to. The formative efforts of the superior will presumably have an effect when they respond to the needs that drew the person into the religious group, but they will not exert much effect when these needs are not being answered.

In recent years this has presented a particularly acute problem in circumstances in which candidates bring with them from the social environment certain values and expectations—maturity, apostolic efficiency, professionalism, attitudes toward authority and obedience —that may or may not be congruent with the formal structure of the religious organization, but which have not been congruent with the attitudes, values, and orientation of the preceding generation of its members and superiors. The ensuing conflict was inevitable, and the unfortunate result was a lessening of attraction to the group among many younger members confronted with this discrepancy.

The problem has been resolved in many instances by a reassessment of group goals and a critical revaluation of the methods of achieving them in concrete situations, and by a recognition of the values deriving from contemporary cultural influences and a gentle modification of them when necessary. When such readjustments can be carried out with the intelligent conviction that there neither is nor need be a contradiction between modern values and the authentic spirit of religious norms, an effective and intelligent solution is possible. It is reasonable to assume that when the religious organization is living up to the most authentic and spiritual values of its founder and institute, it is most effectively responding to and satisfying those individual needs that form the basis of the members' attraction to the organization.

4. The greater the prestige of a group member in the eyes of the other members, the greater the influence he can exert.

This principle is valid for the whole range of group situations. The most obvious source of prestige in the religious group is holding the office of superior, so that the superior is in a preeminent position to influence the members of the group. However, more than one kind of prestige can assert itself in the religious group and, consequently, different dimensions of power that influence the group process and help to form its culture (see Chapter 6).

The more influence a given member exercises, the more prestige and power he enjoys in relation to the other members and the more it may be expected that he will exercise his power responsibly and maturely for the benefit of the group. Any member of a religious group who attains eminence through the exercise of personal gifts and talents has a corresponding obligation to exercise those gifts for the benefit of the group. Although there is a direct proportion between prestige and influence, it is extremely important to bear in mind that every member shares to some extent in the distribution of power in the group, in that he has some capacity to influence and change other members. The group culture through which the forces for change are mediated is a product of the interaction of all members, distributively according to the level of prestige each member enjoys.

In the early novitiate years, the influence of the master or mistress of novices is paramount; this results from the structure of the novitiate situation and also, frequently, from the personal qualities of the master or mistress. It is clear, however, that other forms of prestige, which can exert a positive or a negative effect, may be applicable in the novitiate.

Individuals who have strong personalities or other special gifts will achieve prestige positions quite outside the formal hierarchy of authority. If the master can identify these individuals early, their natural influence can have a positive effect in moving the group toward its goals—here, the specific formational goals of the novitiate. If not, these individuals may become centers of resistance to change as motivated by the master or mistress. It is more likely, in fact, that the strong personalities will assume this function in the group when the discrepancy between those forming and those being formed becomes too great. When such discrepancies occur, it is imperative that communication be maintained as fully as possible so that the corrective process of goal adjustment can operate on both sides.

5. Efforts to change individuals or subparts of a group that, if successful, would result in making them deviate from the norms of the group will encounter strong resistance.

The price of deviation within most groups is rejection. If the individual really desires to be an accepted member of the group, the rejecting pressures can be very effective. An area of religious life in which this finding has special relevance is in special training programs. To meet the demands of apostolic work it is often necessary that individual religious be given highly specialized and technical training. When this is perceived as a deviation within the group, the rejecting forces come into play.

It is not always true that the task-oriented demands of apostolic work are the guiding norms for reactions of individuals within the group. Often, the reaction is dominated by the group's emotionally-oriented inner structure, and when a large percentage of the members become involved in this sort of reaction, the pressures on deviant members can be severe. The effectiveness of such pressures on the deviating individual will be determined by the strength of the emotional system operating in the group, by the personal maturity of the persons participating in it, and by the extent to which task-oriented demands are recognized and accepted by the group. If the group recognizes the special training of an individual as necessary for the attainment of group goals, his position will tend to be seen as less deviant, and less rejecting pressure will be brought to bear.

This depends also on the degree of intelligent task-directedness in the group. If such corrective mechanisms are lacking, the rejecting pressures either will force the individual out of the group or will lead to a situation of heightened tension, aggression toward the group, or formation of subgroups of other members who share his situation or values or both. This type of situation highlights the difficulty that changes in the concrete order can often entail; it also indicates that positive and appropriate change in individuals or in the group can be more readily achieved when the members in question are functioning maturely and intelligently, without excessive involvement in the emotional interaction within the group.

The classic experiment on deviation and rejection was that of Schachter,[5] who was able to show experimentally that a more cohesive group tended to reject a deviant member more strongly and, surprisingly enough, that communications to the member in a deviant role tended to be more frequent. Schachter set up a situation in which there were four kinds of clubs varying in the dimensions of cohesiveness and relevance. Cohesiveness, as we have seen, refers to the members' strength of attraction to the group. Relevance refers to

---

[5] S. Schachter, "Deviation, Rejection, and Communication," *Journal of Abnormal and Social Psycholgoy*, XLVI (1951), 190-207.

a certain activity's degree of importance to the group. The basis of relevance can be the importance of the activity for group locomotion, the value which the group places on the activity, or a relation to certain needs that are more or less common to group members. Each club had five to seven members and there were thirty-two clubs in all. The four divisions were high cohesiveness-relevant issue, low-cohesiveness-relevant issue, high cohesiveness-irrelevant issue, and low cohesiveness-irrelevant issue. Schachter used the following theoretical relations as the basis of his experiment:

1. Pressures to change: pressures acting on group members to change another's deviant opinion to conform more closely with their own.

a. With increasing difference of opinion the magnitude of pressures to change should increase.

b. With increasing cohesiveness, the magnitude of pressures to change should increase. At any point along a scale of difference of opinion, pressures to change should be greater for highly than for lowly cohesive groups.

c. With increasing relevance of issue, the magnitude of pressures to change should increase.

2. Dependence: the extent to which members of a group rely on one another as reference points in establishing social reality (one of the sources of group conformity; see Chapter 3).

a. With increasing difference of opinion the magnitude of dependence will decrease.

b. With increasing cohesiveness, the magnitude of dependence will increase.

c. With relatively small differences of opinion the

magnitude of dependence will increase with increasing relevance of issue. As difference of opinion increases, dependence for relevant issues decreases more rapidly than dependence for irrelevant issues, and a point of zero dependence will be reached with less difference of opinion for relevant than for irrelevant issues.

The group members were classed in three roles: mode, slider, and deviate. The modal role belongs to the members who find themselves in little or no disagreement with the group. The slider is the member who starts in a deviant position and then shifts under group influence toward the modal position. The deviate is, of course, the member whose opinions differ from those of the group.

Within this setting Schachter's experiment was able to demonstrate some interesting findings:

1. Persons in the modal and slider roles will be rejected less (if at all) than will persons in the deviant role.

2. With cohesiveness held constant, rejection will be greater when the issue is relevant than when the issue is irrelevant.

3. With relevance held constant, rejection will be greater in highly cohesive than in lowly cohesive groups.

It can be presumed that in the religious group, the issues that are connected with group goals are relevant to all members of the group. The initial position of the candidate entering the religious group is one of deviance to the group. As the influence of the group comes to bear on him, he must either adopt a modal position and conform to the group standards or shift into the position of the slider. Another of Schachter's findings is that the frequency of communication to the deviate was significantly higher than to the person in the modal position. The other members of the religious group see the deviant position as a discrepancy from their own attitudes, and they set about reducing the strain resulting from such a discrepancy by communication.

This follows the patterns of communication we have already considered (Chapter 2, pp. 36-50). The significant point is that initiation into the religious group is accompanied by strong group pressures to change the candidate in the direction of group attitudes and opinions. The candidate responds by conforming and finding group acceptance or by resisting and suffering the consequences of group rejection. If the cohesiveness of the group is high, these pressures can be especially severe, and unless the other forces attracting the deviate to the group are sufficiently developed, the deviate will find himself separated from the religious group.

The group process thus works toward conformity, but it does so at a price. Not uncommonly, the deviation of the candidate is a reflection of strong and positive potentialities for productivity or imaginative adaptation and leadership that, if brought to maturity, could be of tremendous value to the group in striking the dynamic balance between conformity and adaptation. Thus, although rejection serves to lessen the level of anxiety in the group, it is not always to the ultimate profit of the group.

It seems quite clear that the degree of attraction to the group and the extent to which the individual accepts membership in the group depend on the extent to which the group is able to satisfy the needs of its members.[6] Also, the acceptance of membership in the group depends on the extent to which the values of the group are perceived as compatible with the values of the individual.[7] But these needs are not static, and in the course of time they may change. In the religious group, in fact, the change in needs and values is a part of the formative process. It is not unusual for a candidate for the religious life to be somewhat uncertain about the needs and desires he is seeking to fulfill in entering the religious group. Part of the making of a religious is so to modify his needs that his need structure can find satisfaction within the religious life.

The needs that a person feels are important reflect his value system, and the ultimate discrimination of satisfaction depends on the perception of the compatibility between personal and group values. This can be worked out only by the complex process of communication about the group's purposes and procedures between the individual and the other members of the group. This communication is complemented by a parallel process of evaluation of the individual's activities and a comunication of the group's evaluation to him.

The individual thus receives information about group values, expectancies, symbolic rewards and punishments, evaluations, motivations—the whole complex of information that represents the group culture—from *all* of the other members of the group. Communication occurs at all levels, verbal and nonverbal, explicit and

[6] R. E. Hartley, "Personal Needs and the Acceptance of a New Group as a Reference Group," *Journal of Social Psychology*, LI (1960), 349-58.

[7] R. E. Hartley, "Relationships Between Perceived Values and Acceptance of a New Reference Group," *Journal of Social Psychology* LI (1960), 181-90.

implicit, formal and informal. When interaction among members is sufficient, each individual is provided with a social reality that reinforces approved behavior and inhibits disapproved behavior. Moreover, in the area of needs and values, physical reality is a minimal criterion, so that the individual is left with the social reality of the group as the dominant criterion for judgment and evaluation.

It is possible for the individual to resist these forces operating in the group. Personal factors can complicate the picture. The strength of attraction to the group for a particular member may be relatively weak, with the result that the lessened group influence will be too weak to overcome personal factors running contrary to the group standard. Or it may be that communication between the individual and the rest of the group may be defective and, consequently, that the channels through which group pressure might be brought to bear are closed. In this instance, the individual may be functioning in a deviant position but never really be aware of it.[8]

One of the most intriguing theories for explaining the influence of the group on the individual is Festinger's theory of cognitive dissonance,[9] which asserts that when an individual is confronted by two cognitions that in some way do not fit together, he is led to try to make

[8] L. Festinger, S. Schachter, and K. Black, "The Operation of Group Standards," in D. Cartwright and A. Zander, eds., *Group Dynamics* (Evanston, Ill.: Row, Peterson, 1953), pp. 241-59.
[9] L. Festinger and E. Aronson, "The Arousal and Reduction of Dissonance in Social Contexts," in Cartwright and Zander, *op. cit.*, pp. 214-31. For a critical evaluation of the evidence for this theory, see N. P. Chapenis and A. Chapenis, "Cognitive Dissonance," *Psychological Bulletin*, LXI (1964), 1-22.

them fit together. If the individual must choose among several alternatives, dissonance is almost certain to result, since the chosen alternative is never completely satisfying and the rejected alternatives are never completely repugnant. The more attractive the rejected alternatives are in comparison with the chosen alternative, the more intense will be the dissonance and the greater the effort to resolve it.

Something like this undoubtedly comes into play in the choice of vocation, particularly a religious vocation. The young religious has chosen a way of life that has its good points but at the same time is very demanding and difficult. He has simultaneously rejected another way of life that also has its good points and does not *appear* to be so demanding. When he finds himself living the more difficult life and rejecting the more attractive, he seeks to reduce the dissonance by changing his perception of the life he is trying to lead and heightening the values it represents.

Reduction of dissonance probably plays an important part in changing attitudes and values when the candidate actually begins to participate in the life and activities of the religious community or noviceship. He begins to do things that have their rationale in the purposes and methods proper to the religious life, and the very performance of these acts is most likely somewhat dissonant. The things he does in following the novitiate order of life do not quite fit with his concept of himself —with his attitudes and values, opinions, and so on— which he has developed over the years in constant interaction with people of the world.

The theory of cognitive dissonance has been amply substantiated in situations in which individuals have been forced to perform certain actions or comply with certain norms that were not at the time compatible with their beliefs or opinions. The overt action in opposition to beliefs gives rise to dissonance that the individual can reduce either by stopping the activity or by changing his beliefs to bring them more into line with his external behavior.[10]

In general, the magnitude of the dissonance will depend on the importance of the person or group with whom disagreement is experienced[11] and on the importance and relevance of the issue.[12] If, for example, the religious candidate values group membership highly and is strongly attracted to the group, and if he perceives as important the things about which he finds himself in disagreement, he will be strongly motivated to change his opinions and bring them more into conformity with those of the religious group.

Religious in the period of formation have often felt that their training, particularly in spiritual matters, has been based on the implicit (and sometimes explicit) assumption that when external observance of religious discipline and conformity to observable practices of the religious life are enforced, the young religious is being effectively trained for his future religious life. However, many feel that the emphasis on formalism and externalism in religious life has been excessive and

---

[10] Festinger and Aronson, "The Arousal and Reduction . . . ," in Cartwright and Zander, *op. cit.*, pp. 214-31.
[11] L. Festinger, "Informal Social Communication," *Psychological Review*, LVII (1950), 271-82.
[12] S. Schachter, *The Psychology of Affiliation* (Stanford: Stanford University Press, 1959). See also P. G. Zimbardo, "Involvement and Communication Discrepancy as Determinants of Opinion Conformity," *Journal of Abnormal and Social Psychology*, LX (1960), 86-94.

that correction of the excess is an important area of
adaptation.[13] The object of many such external practices is merely good order in the community. But many
more have formation as their specific objective. Thus,
what is important in their practice is that the internal
dispositions, opinions, and attitudes of the religious be
formed to the group standard.

Undoubtedly, such practices do enlist that power to
change which is provided by cognitive dissonance; if
the candidate continues the practice it is inevitable that
his opinions will change in the desired direction to some
extent. But certain cautions should be urged. First, it
seems that the greater the pressure to enforce the external behavior, the weaker will be the tendency for him
to change his opinion.[14] Second, the motivating force to
reduce dissonance by changing his opinion will extend
only so far as is necessary to reduce the strain caused
by the dissonance. Consequently, there is a point
beyond which reduction of dissonance is ineffective,
although its effectiveness would be extended to the
group and relevance of the issue. Third, the amount of
change that can be expected through reduction of dissonance depends on the amount of justification for acting in conformity with the discrepant position.[15] When
justification is greater, the amount of attitude change
has been shown to be less. One could presume, I think,

---

[13] J. F. Gallen, "Renovation and Adaptation," *Review for Religious,*
XIV (1955), 293-318.
[14] L. Festinger and J. M. Carlsmith, "Cognitive Consequences of
Forced Compliance," *Journal of Abnormal and Social Psychology,*
LVIII (1959), 203-10.
[15] A. R. Cohen, J. W. Brehm, and W. H. Fleming, "Attitude
Change and Justification for Compliance," *Journal of Abnormal and
Social Psychology,* LVI (1958), 276-78.

that the level of justification for external conformity in the context of religious training is high, and, consequently, the effectiveness of reduction of dissonance would be reduced.

The ways in which dissonance is reduced are also fairly well defined. An individual will adopt one of several means for reducing the dissonance. He may try to convince himself that the area of disagreement is not so important after all; he may lessen his valuation of the group or of the person with whom he is in disagreement; he may try to influence the disagreeing other to change his opinion; he may change his own opinion; or he may try to find social support for his position among other members of the group who share his point of view.[16] Any one of these ways is open to the religious.

An area of religious discipline that frequently causes problems in the United States is that of silence. It is difficult to say why this should be so, except that Americans are often very gregarious and conscious of their group membership. They feel a compulsion to communicate, which is very beneficial in many contexts but which often creates problems in the maintenance of proper silence in the religious community. It is the superior's duty to enforce the rule of silence, but the demands of the rule and the dispositions of many religious toward silence create an area of dissonance. If the superior takes steps to enforce silence, he may compound the problem, since the greater his efforts, the more the tendency to reduce the dissonance in the member decreases.

---

[16] Festinger and Aronson, "The Arousal and Reduction . . . ," in Cartwright and Zander, *op. cit.*

Faced with this dissonance, the member may follow the tack of persuading himself that silence is a small matter in the over-all pattern of religious life; as a result, dissonance will be reduced but to the detriment of silence. He may decrease his evaluation of the group, which also decreases dissonance; but this process can have devastating consequences if carried too far. In any case, silence suffers. He may make efforts to alter the stand of the superior in some way: by communication— if the superior permits—he may try to show that the superior's enforcement is too rigid, is causing other kinds of difficulties in the community, and so forth. He may seek out the support of other members of the community who share his views about silence and thus form a subgroup within the community that is to some degree opposed to the superior. This divisive influence is undesirable and it does not help the preservation of silence.

As a final measure, the member can change his own opinion about the rule of silence. The likelihood of this action is increased by the esteem the individual has for the religious group, its goals, and so on, and by the degree to which the rule of silence is perceived by him as an integral part of the organization's structure and an important means to the attainment of its goals. So enforcement of external observance of the rule does not seem to be the best means for bringing about the desired change of attitude; rather, an effort must be made through communication, both formally and informally, to increase the attractive forces on the individual (and, *eo ipso*, the level of cohesiveness in the community), as well as the relevance of the issue. This would reinforce rather than diminish the desired reduction of dissonance. Insistence on external conformity will be effective up to a point, beyond which it begins to have deleterious effects. The initial changes that can be achieved by reducing dissonance between beliefs and external acts must be supplemented by other motivational factors that mere conformism or external control cannot supply.

Another interesting area of application of the principle of cognitive dissonance is that of initiation into the group. Aronson and Mills[17] were able to show that severe initiation into a group tends to increase individuals' liking for the group. According to the theory, by their severe initiation these individuals were impressed with the fact that they had submitted to a painful experience in order to join the group. This cognition was dissonant with the further experience of banal discussion to which they were experimentally subjected. The subjects could reduce this dissonance either by denying the severity of the initiation or, positively, by distorting their perception of group activities; since the initiation was evidently too painful to deny, they seem to have chosen the latter alternative. Such a finding may offer empirical justification for the usual novitiate practices in which the young religious are required to follow a comparatively rigorous regime of mortification, self-denial, and poverty. The demands of such a regime may increase attraction to the group by means of dissonance reduction. But here again it should be noted that dissonance reduction has its limits and demands supplementing by positive motivation.

---

[17] E. Aronson and J. Mills, "The Effect of Severity of Initiation on Liking for a Group," *Journal of Abnormal and Social Psychology*, LIX (1959), 177-81.

The influence of the group in changing the judgment of a particular member will depend on the extent to which the individual relies on the group or on himself as a norm of judgment. Deutsch and Gerard[18] have formulated several principles regarding the relationship between personal judgment and group influence:

1. The influence of group norms on individual judgments will be greater among individuals forming a group than among an aggregation of individuals who do not compose a group.

2. The influence of group norms on individual judgment will be reduced when the individual perceives that his judgment cannot be identified or, more generally, when the individual perceives no pressure to conform directed at himself by others.

Reduction of the group's influence here would stem from a lack of communication. This is a danger in very large religious communities, where a distance is kept between superiors and individual members and where individuals can become lost in the mass, with the result that personal judgment is more or less submerged. When this happens, the influence of group norms decreases.

3. Social influence to conform to one's own judgment will reduce the impact of social influence to conform to the judgment of others.

The influence of the group is not often in the direction of encouraging the following of one's personal judgment, particularly in religious groups. But it is worth noting that it can have this effect.

---

[18] M. Deutsch and H .B. Gerard, "A Study of Normative and Informational Social Influence upon Individual Judgment," *Journal of Abnormal and Social Psychology*, LI (1955), 629-36.

4. Influence to conform to one's own judgment coming from another in addition to from oneself will be stronger than influence merely from oneself.

It is clear from this and from the preceding point that the group influence can act to support the judgment of the individual if it so chooses. This is important when the question of initiative and productivity is raised; there is no intrinsic necessity that the group influence must always be in the direction of conformity. Rather, it would seem that a balance must be struck between group pressures to conform and group pressures to act independently.

5. The more uncertain the individual is about the correctness of his judgment, the more susceptible he will be to group influences in making a judgment.

6. The more uncertain the individual is about the correctness of the judgment of others, the less susceptible he will be to the influence of the group.

Thus, the degree of conformity in the group depends to a certain extent on the degree to which individual members of the group feel that they can rely securely on their own judgment rather than on the group's. In the absence of independent norms of judgment, the individual tends to submit to the pressure of social reality. Social reality is undoubtedly a strong source of such conformity producing pressure in the religious group. But there are other sources that cannot be discounted.

As Cartwright and Zander[19] point out, membership in a group determines many of the things the individual

---

19 D. Cartwright and A. Zander, "Group Pressures and Group Standards," in Cartwright and Zander, *op. cit.*, pp. 165-88.

will see, think about, learn, and do. The restriction in range of experiences tends to make them perceive and do things in a more or less similar manner. It may also be that when some benefit accrues to the group from such conformity the group itself will exert pressures on the individual to conform.

Conformity can serve several functions. It can support the group's attempts to accomplish its goals; it can help the group to continue to maintain itself as a group in the face of disruptive pressures; or it can help members in their attempts to define a context or social climate for their opinions and beliefs. It is important, however, to keep in mind that the pressures exerted by the group toward conformity extend only to matters relevant to the group's activities and the attainment of its goals. This does not exhaust the field of action or opinion open to the member. Even in the religious group, where group goals are so intimately related to the inner convictions and personal needs of members, group pressures operate only in a select area.

One of the most important dimensions of the formative process, which we have touched on in passing, is that of identification. As the individual approaches maturity, he passes through various stages of psychosocial development, during which he constructs the foundations upon which he will build his mature, adult identity.

That identity, which Erikson[20] has spoken of as "ego-identity," involves a complex of personal, social, and cultural factors, all mutually interacting to form and progressively to synthesize the identity of each person.

---

[20] Erikson, *op. cit.*

It would appear to be central to the notion of identity that the individual be able to work out a meaningful and rewarding relationship with each of the important groups within which and in terms of which he is going to find his life adjustment. The success of his relationship to any given group depends upon the extent to which he can fit into a role at once acceptable to the group, rewarded by the group, and congruent with his personal needs. The success of this adjustment depends in turn on the interaction of personality factors with dynamisms within the group, which sets up certain expectancies for the individual members. Some theorists believe that the individual's role function within the group is determined either by group processes or by individual needs,[21] but it seems more reasonable to regard them as interacting.

Some of the types of groups with which the individual interacts have been described by Turner.[22] The "identification group" provides the member with the source of his major perspectives and values. At the opposite extreme of influence is the "interaction group," in which the individual is not personally involved and which merely provides the conditions for certain of his actions. Between these extremes are the "valuation groups," which the individual takes into account only because and insofar as his orientation to the identification group indicates these other groups as reference points. The role that the individual plays in each of these types of

21 F. Redl, "Implications for our Current Models of Personality," in B. Schaffner, ed., *Group Processes: Transactions of the Fourth Conference* (New York: Josiah Macy, Jr., Foundation, 1959), pp. 83-131.
22 R. H. Turner, "Role-Taking, Role Standpoint, and Reference Group Behavior," *American Journal of Sociology*, LXI (1956), 316-28.

group will differ considerably, both in terms of his relation to the group (as adopting a role in relation to the group) and in terms of the expectancies each group will generate for him. These expectancies depend on the nature of the group, the state of its culture, and the degree of centrality of membership the individual undertakes or enjoys.

The most significant relationship is that to the identification group. For the average person, the basic identification groups are family and business. It is within these groups that the average man works out his adult identity. He comes little by little to think of himself as a husband, father, businessman, professional man, or whatever, and the success with which he fulfills these roles is measured by expectancies that are generated within each reference group and derive from cultural influences.

The religious experiences a similar process of adaptation. His or her identification group is obviously the religious group itself, and other interaction and valuation groups will vary to the extent that the religious is placed in contact with them by the demands of apostolic activity. For the religious teaching in a grammar school, the primary valuation group would be the faculty of the school or the class itself. This activity may demand peripheral dealings with book publishers, teachers' organizations, and so forth. For the religious teaching at the level of secondary or higher education, the primary valuation group may be the professional group rather than the educational institution. This can constitute another source of tension for the religious with professional or specialized training. Included in the objective of graduate training is the socialization of the student to the end that the professional group becomes his identification group.

Such influences are an inevitable part of graduate training, but they can create a dilemma for the religious whose identification is already firmly established within the religious group. The real problem in such a situation is not participation in activities proper to the respective groups; it is, rather, the conflict in personal identity of the religious person himself.

It seems quite clear that groups do distinguish between roles for their members. In small groups, for example, it has been shown that the group tends to differentiate the functions of task accomplishment and external goal accomplishment from the more internal functions of group integration and expression.[23] This seems to parallel Bion's distinction between task-orientation and emotionality-orientation. This has important implications for leadership (see Chapter 6), but at the moment we are concerned with specialization in the functions of the members.

The functioning of members tends to differentiate along lines of inner group integration as opposed to outer-directed task accomplishment. Thus, members who are well liked by other members seem to have a need to be liked, to the extent that they will actually forego opportunities for task-oriented activity because of the threat it may pose to their personal relationships. Avoidance of controversy and harmony are their staples, with the consequence that they may retire into the conventional security of the mediocre performer. On the

---

[23] P. E. Slater, "Role Differentiation in Small Groups," *American Sociological Review*, XX (1955), 300-10.

other hand, members whose task performance level is high may well assume such a role because of an unwillingness or inability to respond to the needs of others. Such members' compulsive involvement in external work may serve as a shield against the anxiety created by becoming involved in the needs of others. These tendencies represent extremes, but the significant factor is that the group process contributes to the tendency of each pattern to be more or less strong in proportion to the distribution of tendencies in the group to work or emotionality.

When tendencies to emotionality predominate, the liking extreme tends to play a greater part; when tendencies to work are prevalent, the influence of tendencies to task performance is greater. The manner in which these group tendencies affect individuals will depend on the personality characteristics of the individuals. The interaction works both ways; the group induces individuals of suitable disposition into one or other role, and individuals of particular characteristics tend to gravitate toward the congenial role.

All of this is immediately relevant to the problem of religious formation. We can regard the process of formation as an interaction between individual personality and group forces that is calculated to help the young religious solve the problems of adjustment to the religious life and attain a mature sense of his or her own identity as a religious. Often (more and more often in our times) there is added to this the need of developing an identity as a professional specialist.

In the growth to maturity, the years in which the young religious is undergoing formation (late teens and, early twenties) are the critical years for the decisive formation of identity. Failure to follow the natural course of personality growth to identity during these years can have devastating consequences. If the religious group does not set up the conditions under which proper growth toward maturity, responsibility, assimilation of group values, positive identification with the group, personal reward and fulfillment are not only possible but also positively fostered, it is failing in its basic responsibility to God, to the Church, and to its members.

Although it is true that certain practices can interfere with the growth to mature identity, it is also true that no specific practices can force identity when the prior potentiality for it is missing. The religious group must use the best means available to assure that the members it accepts will be mature young people with the capacity for growth. In recent years, the application and continued improvement of testing procedures, the use of psychological tests as screening devices, psychiatric interviews in certain instances, and a generally growing awareness of the importance of personality factors in the religious life have contributed significantly to the selection of candidates. There is every reason to believe that progress in selection will continue. But even the normal and well-adjusted young man or woman has not reached the level of mature personality growth. For the success of the individual's religious life and the effective functioning of the group as a whole, it is imperative that the full potentialities of each individual become actualized during the course of formation. If growth to mature identity is inhibited, the consequences must be paid for in anxiety, insecurity, lack of self-esteem, basic uncertainty, and an impairment of responsibility.

Much could be said about the intrapsychic aspects of the personality that has failed to achieve an identity. Erikson has elaborated the condition in terms of "identity diffusion,"[24] but here we are more directly concerned with the resulting dynamic patterns between the individual and the group. The correlate of defective identity is an emotionality that causes the individual to react excessively to emotional influences in his environment. Human interaction is always compounded with emotional interaction. Consequently, the person who lacks maturity will follow one or another of the basic assumptions that Bion has pointed out. He will become deeply involved in the internal system (Homans) of the group, either by growing excessively dependent and, therefore, incapable of responsible and independent action (dependence); or by reacting rebelliously to group pressures (fight); or by taking refuge in outside interests or even task-oriented activities approved by the group where personal interaction is minimized (flight); or by setting up mutually supportive and protective relationships with individual members of the group (pairing). His basic tendency to impulsive acting-out rather than to intelligent inquiry and task-oriented seeking of reality[25] has a disruptive effect on the efficiency and effectiveness of the group.

The basic anxiety of the person with a defective identity leads him often to the development of socially

---

[24] Erikson, *op. cit.*
[25] See discussion of Thelen's theory in Chapter 2.

structured defense mechanisms. The basic notion under-lying a socially structured defense mechanism is that individuals project into objective reality and externalize their own characteristic psychic defense mechanisms. In time, a social defense system develops through the interaction, and often unconscious agreement, among the members of the organization. This requires interaction between individuals who are motivated to reduce the anxiety stemming from the insecurity of a defective identity. The situation can develop to the point where the socially structured defense mechanism is regarded as an aspect of the objective reality of the group life to which both old and new members must adjust.

One important area in which this type of mechanism operates is that of responsibility. Defective identity bears with it a certain element of impulsiveness that is quite readily seen as irresponsibility. This is especially true in a setting in which a high premium is placed on responsibility. The individual is bound to develop a severe attitude toward these impulses, which can readily be reinforced in an atmosphere that stresses the obligations of responsibility. The individual whose identity is not sufficiently developed to integrate these aspects of the personality structure will embark on a process of denial, splitting-off, and projection that will externalize the irresponsible impulses and attribute them to his or her inferiors; at the same time the severe attitudes toward such irresponsibility are externalized and attributed to his or her superiors. Such an indi-vidual will perceive his or her inferiors as impulsive and irresponsible, and this will constitute the objective reality regardless of the general pattern of behavior among the inferiors. The same individual will perceive the actions of superiors as harsh and demanding, and this, too, will represent the objective reality. In other words, juniors are irresponsible and superiors are harsh disciplinarians precisely because the individual has assigned them such roles.

Let us go a step further. If individual inferiors have not yet achieved mature identity, they will become involved in the same process; not only will they perceive the original subject as a harsh superior, but also he, as a superior, will in fact tend to become precisely that because he has projected his own irresponsible self on to his inferiors. Similarly, if the member's individual superior is not a person of mature identity, he too will be caught in the same process of projection and externalization. Thus, inherent impulsiveness at all levels of the hierarchy of authority can set up a social defense system based on the socially structured defense mechanisms of anxious individuals at each level. The mechanisms are mutually reinforcing. But we can carry the implications even further.

At each step, the operation of a socially structured defense mechanism creates roles and assigns them to others, both inferiors and superiors. The "psychic truth" of the individual's projection tends to become an objective truth because people do, in fact, tend to act and respond in terms of the roles assigned to them. When this stage is reached the circle is closed and all segments are mutually reinforcing.

The intensity with which such a social defense system can operate depends on the level of mature identity development among the individuals concerned. However, attitudes toward responsibility can be quite influential. Menzies[26] describes the operation of such a social defense system in a British nursing service, where responsibility for patient care is quite high. A strong emphasis and a high premium is often placed on responsibility in religious groups. This is particularly true of the superior, upon whom the major burden of responsibility for the accomplishment of goal tasks and for the personal well-being and perfection of the members is frequently imposed. It is not difficult to imagine the effect of this emphasis on that superior who does not feel secure in the acceptance and handling of responsibility and who does not possess an adequate sense of his identity as a responsible religious and superior. Unless both his superiors and his inferiors are mature and autonomous individuals, who are able to resist collusive involvement in his socially structured defense, the social defense system is certain to develop. The consequences will be dissatisfaction, grumbling, criticism, decreased efficiency and effectiveness of the group, resulting from the diversion of energies from task involvement to the emotional involvement of the defense system, and so forth.

When such a system involves young religious who are still in formation, a twofold deficit is added: (1) the interaction of the defense system has a strong influence in shaping the attitudes of such young religious toward the superior-inferior relationship in religious life; and (2) to the extent that individuals become involved in such a system, it impairs their own

---

[26] I. E. P. Menzies, "A Case-Study in the Functioning of Social Systems as a Defense Against Anxiety," *Human Relations,* XIII (1960), 95-121.

eventful growth to maturity. The effect of such a system on the young is all the more intense because they are at a critical stage of their development when the crisis of identity must be faced. Further, an especially strong emphasis on the responsibility of superiors for the training and formation of young religious is not uncommon. Although such an emphasis is quite prudent over-all, under the circumstances we have been discussing it risks reinforcing the tendency of the social defense system to form. When this happens, the result will be a tendency on the superior's part to be overanxious about the fulfillment of his responsibility and a corresponding tendency on the part of the members to respond to the implicit expectation that they function immaturely and irresponsibly.

In the modern context, the increasing apostolic pressures on religious groups require an ever-increasing level of professional training. As these demands intensify, the need for intelligent and mature religious personnel is magnified. A different set of values is called into operation as a result of progressive specialization of roles and functions within the religious group. The premium is put on productivity rather than comfortable mediocrity, on initiative rather than conformity, on maturity and independence of judgment rather than on dependence, and so forth. Such a shift in values demands a spiritual formation that is intelligent and mature and that permits the full potential of growth for the individual. It requires a spirituality in which the basic notions of service and apostolicity are given greater play.[27]

---

[27] See J. H. Fichter's pregnant remarks on the adaptation of formation for the modern apostolate in *Religion as an Occupation* (Notre Dame, Ind.: University of Notre Dame Press, 1961), pp. 88-112.

It has not been the purpose here to make specific suggestions or recommend changes in existing practices. From our considerations thus far it should be evident that too much depends on the special characteristics of each group and the level of maturity of its members for specific recommendations to have much merit. The purpose has been to create a sense of how the group process affects the formative process. If intelligent adaptation is to take place in religious formation, it must be sought with an awareness of all the factors that determine its effectiveness. Consequently, the functions of the group itself cannot be discounted, since they have the power in themselves, regardless of organizational procedures or factors of personality, to make or break the formative process.

5

Personal Initiative and the
Group Process

The importance of personal initiative in the religious life has increased as environmental pressures and demands on the religious groups have increased. As the apostolic works of religious groups have diversified and intensified in recent years, the opportunities and the necessity for independent and responsible action on the part of individual religious have multiplied. With the rising crescendo in external demands, it has become less and less possible for a particular religious to take refuge in the security and anonymity of community life. There was a time when such self-effacement could pass for an ideal, but in our time it must more often be regarded as a partial failure of the religious life and as a crippling of the apostolic effectiveness of the religious group.

At the same time, for the preservation of the group life it is absolutely essential that members conform to the demands and expectations of the religious group. We have considered this aspect of conformity under the rubric of formation, since, from the group standpoint, the formative process is aimed at a change of attitudes to conform with the values, attitudes, standards, and expectations of the group. Group pressures operate quite effectively to fit the young candidate into the group structure. The success of the process depends on the extent to which the group has importance to the young religious, on the strength of the forces that attract him to the group, on the level of cohesiveness in the group, on the degree to which group goals are valued by the members, and so on.

All of these elements are, within limits, positive factors in the maintenance of the group and in facilitating group locomotion toward its goals. We have also seen that when and if the individual member perseveres in a deviant role, the group has resources for preserving uniformity, that is, by redefining the boundaries of the group to exclude the deviant member. This process is more likely to occur when the factors reinforcing group uniformity are stronger.

A certain degree of uniformity is essential to the group process insofar as it reduces confusion and wasted effort and produces an orderliness that contributes to the group's over-all effectiveness. However, if such pressures become too strong, they can cause uneasiness, rigidity and inflexibility, and a reduction of creativity and productivity in individual members.[1] Consequently, there is an ideal balance attainable between those pressures toward uniformity that promote and support the group process and the personal needs of the members for the exercise of responsibility, initiative, and independence.

---

[1] D. Cartwright and A. Zander, "Group Pressures and Group Standards," in Cartwright and Zander, eds., *Group Dynamics* (Evanston, Ill.: Row, Peterson, 1953), pp. 165-88.

The degree to which group pressures affect members varies over a considerable range. Berkowitz[2] has shown experimentally that members of a group who regard themselves as dependent on it for attaining their personal goals become much more strongly motivated toward the group task than members who can achieve their goals independently. This leaves the question why dependent members should become or perceive themselves as dependent. It also appears that members who feel more accepted in the group tend to feel freer to think for themselves and to deviate from the group standards.[3]

This finding seems to indicate that those aspects of the formative process for young religious that undermine the sense of being a bona fide member of the religious group have a correlative effect of reinforcing conformity. Presumably, the young religious who is attracted to the group but does not feel accepted by it would tend to conform as a means of gaining acceptance. Under conditions of nonacceptance, however, this conformity diminishes the strength of attraction to the group and the power of the group to effect change in the individual. Continued nonacceptance has the effect of increasing external conformity and decreasing the internal motivation for substantial growth in the religious spirit. On the other hand, increased acceptance will have the converse effect of deemphasizing con-

---

[2] L. Berkowitz, "Effects of Perceived Dependency Relationships upon Conformity to Group Expectations," *Journal of Abnormal and Social Psychology*, LV (1957), 350-54.

[3] J. Jackson and H. Saltzstein, "The Effect of Person-Group Relationships on Conformity Processes," *Journal of Abnormal and Social Psychology*, LVII (1958), 17-24.

formity and simultaneously reinforcing tendencies to personal initiative and independence.

In general, it seems that marginal group members, whose position in the group is more or less peripheral and whose status is not secure, tend to show a very high degree of conformity but lack the high degree of attraction to the group of members who are in a position of secure, high acceptance.[4] Hollander[5] has pointed out that the increase of group acceptance through observation of the individual's performance and general characteristics tends to build up a sort of "idiosyncratic credit" that permits him a wider range of deviant or independent activity.

Consequently, the higher one's status and acceptance in the group, the more freedom the group concedes for activities that do not strictly conform to its standards. But if the individual exceeds the amount of credit that the group concedes him, the pressures to uniformity in the group will begin to be mobilized. The point at which an individual passes the line of permissible "idiosyncrasy" and assumes a position of deviance will depend on the degree of acceptance, on the extent to which the sources of pressure to uniformity are active in the group and contribute to its goal locomotion, and so forth. It is often the case, as we have had occasion to remark in regard to specialization in religious groups, that the group creates specialized positions that carry with them a specific set of responsibilities and func-

---

[4] L. Berkowitz and J. R. Macaulay, "Some Effects of Differences in Status Level and Status Ability," *Human Relations*, XIV (1961), 135-48.

[5] E. P. Hollander, "Conformity, Status, and Idiosyncrasy Credit," *Psychological Review*, LXV (1958), 117-27.

tions. Members filling these positions are supposed to act in a way prescribed by the group's expectations for those positions.

Within the religious group the specialist in any field is expected to comport himself with religious modesty even while he fulfills a function that places him in a position of prestige, A special pattern of adjustment corresponding to a special set of expectations generated by the group is called for. These role prescriptions constitute a form of pressure toward uniformity that results from the group's adaptation to diversification of function. If the individual does not conform to these expectations, he will be subjected to group pressures to conform as long as he is within the limits of his idiosyncrasy credit or he will be excluded when he exceeds this credit.

The degree of conformity increases as we move toward the periphery of any group, that is, as we move from the positions of higher to lower status. At the outer fringe, however, another gradient asserts itself to increase the level of nonconforming behavior.[6] It should be obvious that lack of conformity at the lower status level differs from lack of conformity at the higher level. Although lack of conformity at the higher level may or may not be equivalent to the deviation, it is almost always equivalent to deviation at the lower status level. Presumably, the forces of attraction and valuation of group goals are diminished at this status level so that deviant behavior is more frequently a form of rebellion than otherwise.

---

[6] O. J. Harvey and C. Consalvi, "Status and Conformity to Pressure in Informal Groups," *Journal of Abnormal and Social Psychology*, LX (1960), 182-87.

This means that conforming behavior in the religious group is most probable among those members who do not have sufficient ego strength or independence of judgment to determine their own course of action and thought but who at the same time are bound to the group by strong attractive forces. The forces of attraction are rooted in deep personal needs that membership in the group satisfies. If the forces of attraction are decreased by any of the mechanisms we have discussed previously (see Chapter 3), the pattern of conformity will be broken. It is also quite clear that an individual member can conform in certain areas and act entirely independently in others, depending on the differential pressures within the community and the selectivity of his personal needs.

Another important group influence on the pattern of independence and conformity stems from the group's mode of organization. The bureaucratic mode of organization aims at the systematic coordination of the work of many individuals. Even though the religious community is basically a primary group in which the functioning of the group is in terms of face-to-face relations, it is still a functioning part of a larger organization that tends to operate along bureaucratic lines (see Chapter 1). Fichter[7] has synthesized the essential aspects of the bureaucratic mode of organization as follows:

1. The typical bureaucracy has an orderly, hierarchical *centralization of power* in which the grades of authority can be traced upward and downward.

---

[7] J. H. Fichter, S.J., "The Sociological Aspects of the Role of Authority in the Adaptation of the Religious Community for the Apostolate," in Joseph E. Haley, C.S.C., ed., *1958 Sisters' Institute of Spirituality* (Notre Dame, Ind.: University of Notre Dame Press, 1959), pp. 46-47.

2. The bureaucracy *emphasizes rules,* procedures, patterns, which have become formalized from frequent and traditional repetition.

3. The secret of efficiency in the bureaucracy is the specialization and *simplification of individual tasks* because each task is seen only as one segment of the whole.

4. Relatively *little initiative* is allowed to the individuals in the bureaucratic form of organization.

5. In the bureaucracy there tends to be a *corporate responsibility* in the sense that it is the system itself, as a whole, that gets the work done.

6. *Impersonality* is also a frequent characteristic of the bureaucracy.

7. The status of the person is mainly a *status of ascription;* since the relative position of any person is fixed on an organizational basis, the prestige any person enjoys is mainly the prestige of the office he holds and only secondarily the result of personal qualities and achievement.

8. Finally, in a bureaucracy emphasis is placed on the fact that the *individual* serves the organization.

Although these characteristics can be applied readily to the religious organization, the religious group has been forced to modify its mode of operation and organization because of the growing number of religious whose training and orientation are professional. The professional mode of organization is characterized by the following emphases:[8]

---

[8] *Ibid.,* pp. 48-49.

1. In the professional type of organization there tends to be a diffused *leadership of expertness.*

2. The professional system of organization necessarily *allows variability* in the sense that the functionary must be guided by the rules of the function rather than by the rules of the organization.

3. The task of the professional *cannot be simplified* and routinized.

4. The professional form of organization *encourages initiative* in the individual.

5. This kind of system places *personal responsibility* upon the professional who can be readily identified as the one who performs the central tasks.

6. The professional type of organization calls for *good personal relations* among the members.

7. The prestige of the professional worker is primarily an *achieved status* rather than an ascribed status.

8. In the professional organization attention is focused on the fact that the *worker serves the client.*

In a period when the functions of the religious group were fairly homogeneous and the demands of the social environment were simple enough that the performance of functions at a somewhat amateur level could be regarded as adequate, the bureaucratic mode of organization was the preferred system for the efficient performance of tasks. In recent times, however, the functions of the religious group have become considerably more heterogeneous and diversified, and in many instances they have been raised to a level of performance that necessitates professional training of a high order.

Because of the rising standards of performance in society, even functions that the religious with a general background could handle quite adequately a few years ago now demand professional training. This phenomenon is not restricted to religious personnel but affects all modern professions. A doctor with the training of his colleagues of a generation ago would not be able to obtain a license today. Consequently, the bureaucratic mode of organization is no longer the most efficient and preferred orientation. But the religious group cannot adopt a completely professional organization and expect to maintain itself as a religious group. The answer obviously lies in a compromise solution[9] in which the bureaucratic elements essential to the functioning of a large organization are integrated with those aspects of a professional organization that enable the religious functionary to work effectively in the pursuit of his specialized task.

The alternatives are clear-cut. If the religious group adopts a rigid bureaucratic stance, it will have to retire from the modern apostolate. If it accepts a half-hearted compromise, in which its members are asked to function as professionals while the functioning of the group remains dominantly bureaucratic, the price must be paid in defections, tepidity, anxiety, frustration, and inefficiency. The only possible alternative is that the group modify its structure and its culture so that the demands of the professional orientation can be confronted competently.

---

[9] *Ibid.*, pp. 50-51. See also J. H. Fichter's *Religion as an Occupation* (Notre Dame, Ind.: University of Notre Dame Press, 1961), pp. 226-33.

The extent to which such adjustment can be achieved successfully depends on the group's motivation to adapt to the demands of its external tasks. With sufficient feedback and adequate communication within the group, such modifications should not present any great difficulty. When the emotionality-oriented inner system is dominant, however, or when the security of crucial individuals is further threatened by impending changes, the process of adaptation can be impeded. The importance of adaptation cannot be overemphasized, since what is at stake is not merely segmented areas of function but basic attitudes and values and psychological dispositions. Consequently, adjustment must extend to all aspects of organizational functioning. This can be spelled out further in terms of the differing characteristics of the two modes of organization.

1. Centralized leadership versus leadership of expertness. In a more simple cultural context, the religious group accentuated to a much greater extent the leadership of authority. There were always some individuals whose high prestige and influence in the group derived from expertness, but for the most part they were exceptions who did not interfere with the group's basic bureaucratic structure. More often than not, the superior could maintain his position of leadership because he also held a relatively high position in the hierarchy of skills and competencies that the group and the culture valued highly. He knew as much or more than any of his members about the problems of the group's apostolic work, and his competence in areas of general knowledge could be favorably compared with any other member of the community. To a great extent he was able to combine

the leadership of authority with a leadership of expertness.

The radical complexity of the culture and the increasing demand for specialization in the performance of apostolic functions have changed this picture. The superior can no longer assume that his competence extends equally to all important areas of community life. If the modern superior leans too much upon his own judgment, he runs the risk of working counter to the leadership of expertness, which no longer resides in himself but in his community. If he retreats to the authoritarian stance that expertness must yield to authority—presuming there is conflict between the two—he not only diminishes his own prestige and influence in the community, but he also creates tensions and conflicts for members possessing expert qualifications. In actuality, he would be forcing them into a position of infantile dependence that directly violates their sense of personal responsibility.

It follows that in many instances—which are likely to increase as time goes on—the superior in a religious community functions less in the role of authoritarian order-giver, and more and more as director of the cooperative activities of the members of his community. More and more he must rely on the expert advice and opinions of his members, which means that the area of responsibility open to them is expanded. Moreover, although the area of expanded responsibility is opened by the expert, it must extend also to the other members of the community. A whole new atmosphere and an entirely new set of attitudes of members of the group toward the superior-member relationship must be formed. The presence of professional values in the community sets this process moving, so that the superior can operate effectively only if he adapts his mode of operation to the new situation.

It is essential in this discussion of the exercise of authority that there be no confusion regarding the essential structure of the religious community. The locus of legitimate authority in the community is the superior, and that authority cannot be communicated to any other member of the community. It is an essential part of religious life that a primary polarity exist between superior and members structured around the superior's authority and the member's obedience.

It should also be quite clear that the polarity of authority-obedience should not determine the distribution of responsible activity within the community. If the religious cannot assume or exercise legitimate authority, there is no reason why he cannot accept and exercise responsible activity through cooperation with the superior, through the exercise of certain functions in the name of the superior, or through the superior's delegation. There is a real distinction between the exercise of responsible activity and leadership, on the one hand, and the exercise of authority on the other.

2. Emphasis on rules versus variability. One of the dominant characteristics of religious group life is the esteem and high valuation of the formalized rules by which the operations of the group and the lives of the individual members are directed. The rules make explicit how the member may achieve personal sanctification and the fullness of religious life. At the same time, they are human conventions that require constant reinterpretation (less frequently, reformulation) to meet the changing demands of the situation. The abstract norm

proposed by the rule is to be fulfilled concretely according to the judgment of mature prudence. Rigid adherence to one or other legitimate interpretation or an excessive clinging to the letter of the law is normally neither mature nor prudent.

The mature religious realizes that the legislator cannot and does not intend to legislate for every conceivable situation. Consequently, it is up to the member to fulfill the spirit of the rule as far as possible and in accord with the norms of reasonable and prudent judgment. As long as the bureaucratic mode was supreme and the area of personal responsibility was at a minimum, the strong emphasis on strict observance of the rules followed naturally. The legalistic attitude thus generated found a rigid and voluntaristic interpretation of the law quite congenial. But as a strictly bureaucratic mode of functioning has more and more become passé, the use of individual prudential judgment and the adoption of a more flexibly rationalistic attitude toward the law have gained greater acceptance. Consequently, there is an element of indeterminacy that can cause anxiety in the obsessively disposed superior and/or member, but it is an indeterminacy that can only be met by the free and mature response of the individual religious. The emphasis must shift from dependence to autonomy within the limits of the spirit of the law and the demands of adaptation.

3. Simplification of tasks versus totality of tasks. The breakdown of tasks into simpler operational elements and the ritualization of task-performance are possible in situations where personal judgment and decision can be kept to a minimum. Making a decision implies a choice among possible courses of action. This choice is

attended by a certain amount of uncertainty concerning the outcome and, consequently, by a certain amount of conflict and anxiety. Ritualization serves to eliminate the decision process and so to diminish anxiety. If anxiety tolerance is low, this sort of ritualization can serve as a defense, but if ritualization does achieve this secondary end, it does so at the cost of abandoning personal responsibility and initiative.

The type of task that the professional person undertakes is a professional task precisely insofar as it requires judgment and decision by a person trained specifically to deal with this kind of problem. Ritualization is impossible, and, consequently, the professional person must inevitably exercise his personal responsibility in carrying out his work. The group within which the professional person functions is forced to face the relative indeterminacy and insecurity that it had previously been able to avoid by simplification of function and ritualization. If the administration cannot tolerate this indeterminacy and insists on some form of ritualization, the professional is immersed in a conflict that demands the sacrifice of his efficiency and effectiveness, with the result that the judgment which is properly his responsibility as a professional person will be taken out of his hands.

The problem includes more than strictly professional activities, since responsibility itself is at stake. It is not psychologically meaningful to speak of a person as responsible in one area and irresponsible in another. Responsibility is a property of the person and it is he who acts in all his actions. As a result, one cannot demand infantile dependence in one direction and responsibility in another. The professional religious must be or become a more responsible religious in all phases of his religious life. Although it would be rash to push conclusions too far without well-established evidence to back them up, one wonders what effect this characteristic simplification and ritualization of tasks in religious houses of formation would have on the mature religious' later functioning as a professional person.

4. Deemphasis of initiative versus emphasis of initiative. This tension touches at the core of the present chapter's consideration. In a bureaucratic setting, simplification of procedures, ritualization, the emphasis on obedience and submission, authoritarian leadership, and other factors have a tendency to leave little room for the development or exercise of initiative. The critical question for the group is whether initiative is to be valued or devalued in terms of propelling the group toward its goals. If it is devalued, group pressures will work to minimize initiative; if it is valued, group pressures to uniformity will be modified to permit and even encourage initiative. Initiative will be shown only by a personality ready to accept the repsonsibility for its nonuniform action and in circumstances in which initiative is rewarded rather than censured.

Even if an individual were disposed to show initiative and creativity by means of his own personality and ability, the group can effectively block that disposition by the exercise of punitive pressures. At one time it was necessary that initiative in the religious community be somewhat devalued, both as disruptive of established patterns and as purely deviant behavior. With the diversification of tasks that marks the modern religious community, the range for acceptable initiative has multiplied accordingly, and the impulse to take initiative has been intensified with the introduction of a professional orientation.

Initiative is as much opposed to merely deviant behavior as it is to excessively conforming behavior. Deviant behavior is exercised through opposition to or rejection of group goals; true initiative is exercised as an effort to improve or implement group goals according to improved methods and techniques. Thus, the extent to which the group accepts and values initiative will depend on all the factors involved in readjusting the group according to the goals it has set and the methods it plans to use for achieving those goals. Defects in task-orientation, in communication, in feedback, in group cohesiveness will have a hurtful influence on the exercise of initiative. This is important for the professional member of the group, since his personal initiative is essential to carry out his task effectively. The group process can either support him or impair his efficiency.

The individual member may never be aware of the pressures within the group that are important in determining the amount or the kind of initiative shown. As we shall see, initiative is in part a manifestation of certain personality characteristics, but the great temptation for the individual is to perceive the problem only in these terms. The individual who is gifted with exceptional ego-strength and who places a high value on initiative will be able to maintain interest and productivity in his apostolic work over the course of years. But such individuals are rare, and the likelihood is that members of the group who have not developed such self-reliance and independence will find themselves falling into the anxiety-alleviating pattern of ritualization of their lives. Their ambitions are dashed, their interests lose fire, their apostolic efforts become mere routine, they tend increasingly to avoid decisions and responsibility, they become less and less concerned with receiving feedback information from the social environment—the best means of adaptation for maintaining or increasing apostolic effectiveness—they slide into a state of mind in which conformity and routine are valued more than initiative and the exercise of personal judgment.

The phenomenon is not restricted to members of religious groups; it is a rather general characteristic of the aging segments of all groups. This is not an indictment of conservatism, but it is an indictment of that kind of conservatism which kills initiative and personal responsibility at the same time that it impedes apostolic effectiveness. The adaptation motivating the person who follows this pattern arises from the need to avoid the anxiety that stems either from the uncertainty entailed in making decisions and accepting responsibility or from the more subtle influences deriving from the group.

If the group does not value initiative, if the group is not secure with the distribution of responsibility, if the group does not support and accept individual attempts to show initiative, personal ego resources will hold out only to a certain point, at which the individual will abandon the attempt. If the group does not value the individual's contribution and does not offer him any rewards in terms of recognition or prestige, the pressures to uniformity will take their toll. This is especially true in groups in which the tendency to emotionality is strong; initiative has no meaning except in relation to goal locomotion or task performance, and in either case initiative will force realignments within the group culture that the emotional system tolerates only with difficulty.

5. Corporate responsibility versus personal responsibility. In a professional setting, responsibility for the success or failure of the task belongs to the professional workers, and both the professional and those whom he serves recognize this fact. It is not uncommon in the religious group, however, that there is a certain amount of obscurity about who is responsible to whom and for what. The ritualization of tasks, which is so common in houses of formation and which tends to be carried over into apostolic works (for example, simplification and ritualization in the priestly ministry are carried to the point at which in most instances it does not make any difference who the priest is as long as he is a priest), tends to remove the burden of responsibility from the members and pass it to superiors.

This is reinforced by the social-defense mechanism of projecting to superiors attitudes concerning responsibility or the lack of it (see Chapter 4). The result is not only an abandonment of responsibility by the members, but also a trend toward relegating more complex and difficult tasks to higher levels in the hierarchy of authority. As a consequence, members sometimes end up performing tasks that are far below their capacity, while their superiors are burdened with too many complex activities. The effectiveness of both suffers.

No clear-cut solution can be offered for distribution of responsibility. Much depends on the nature of the group and the type of function it performs. Some groups expect all members to assume as much responsibility as possible; other groups concentrate the responsibility in one person and exclude other members from sharing in it. It is often thought that the concentration of responsibility increases efficiency. Undoubtedly, efficiency is served by such an arrangement when the withdrawal of responsibility from lower levels can help in the performance of the task, that is, in the kind of simplified and ritualized procedures referred to above. But when the worker's responsibility is an essential element in the situation, efficiency may well suffer when responsibility is withdrawn.

It is obvious that not everyone in a group can have a final say about the way things are done; the result of such a policy would be administrative chaos. But it is also clear that the concentration of responsibility undermines motivation and morale, destroys creativity, and produces conflicts, frustration, and hostility between members and superiors.[10] Granted that the acceptance and exercise of responsibility is a function of a mature personality, it is not unreasonable to expect that whatever the formal structure of authority within the group the individual should exercise personal responsibility within the area of his contribution to the group's performance. Without avoiding his own responsibility, the superior can delegate certain of his functions to lower levels in the authority hierarchy, thus providing a better distribution of responsible activity. He can, and in the modern context often must, accept a larger measure of cooperative dependence on the judgment and knowledgeability of his members.

In short, there is a balance that can be struck between the anxiety-reductive concentration of responsibility on

[10] D. Cartwright and A. Zander, "Leadership and Group Performance: Introduction," in Cartwright and Zander, *op. cit.,* p. 505.

the one hand and administrative chaos on the other. The formal structure of the system is important, but it is not the most important facet of the problem. The religious community functions to a large extent as a primary, informal group. Consequently, attitudes and personal needs have a greater impact on the group culture. In the matter of responsibility, the most important factor is the prevailing attitude toward it. The formal structure that concentrates responsibility can often produce an attitude that places a high value on this type of distribution. But informal steps can be taken to foster and encourage the acceptance of responsibility and—without violating the formal structure—spread the task of responsible action over a wider range of group members. The superior does not abandon his responsibility when he reduces his active range of actual function (see Chapter 6).

6. Impersonal relations versus personal relations. The relationship between superior and member in the religious group is too often characterized by a certain impersonality. This may result from an insecurity in the superior, in the subject, or in both that makes warm interpersonal contacts difficult. Or it may be a result of attitudes toward the superior-member relationship that have been generated within the bureaucratic structure. The value of the task and its performance is maximized, and the value of the person performing it is minimized. This has the administrative advantage of reducing sentimentality and favoritism, but it has the disadvantage of constantly impressing on the individual that he is not valued as a person and that the system can very well get along without him. Many aspects of common life tend to underline a kind of impersonal status

of the individual vis-à-vis the group: identical clothing, denial of personal possessions, etc. This emphasis can be reinforced considerably by a rigid adherence of superiors to the unwritten law that permission should not be given to one unless it can easily be given to all.

When the simplification of task procedures guaranteed the effective performance of group functions, the group could pay the price in deterioration of individual personalities with the assurance that paying the price would buy the achievement of group goals. The time-honored themes of sacrifice and dedication to God's work were built into a rationalization of such depersonalizing attitudes. This was not always a guarantee that the work would be done, but the value of the system was reinforced by the consoling thought that the reason the holy brother cook ruined the community's dinner was that he was caught up in the contemplation of divine things.

The community may have been able to put up with inferior cooking, but modern culture demands—and has every right to expect—professional service, and the community can no longer put up with inferior performance of apostolic tasks. The effective performance of professional services demands the mature functioning and responsible activity of the professional worker. One cannot expect the individual to maintain the quality of creative and productive work over any extended period unless he is made to feel that his personal contribution is valued by the community, not merely tolerated. He must be made to feel that he has a place and function within the community that is uniquely his and that to some extent the success of the community's functioning is his personal responsibility. Rather than an impersonal cog in a massive machine, he must feel that he is an intelligent human cooperator and contributor in the group's movement toward its goals.

I believe that what is most essential in this orientation can be expressed in terms of identity and identification. The effective operation of the professional person (and the important point is that the religious, exclusive of any subsidiary professional commitment, *is* a professional person) demands that he possess a well-developed sense of his identity as a human being and as a professional functionary. It is essential to the mature functioning of the religious person, therefore, that he possess a mature sense of his own religious identity, an important element of which is identification with the religious group. It is psychologically impossible for a person with a mature personal identity to identify with a group in which he is regarded and treated as an impersonal and unimportant cog.

Such identification can only be at the cost of regression from personal maturity and a loss of personal identity. The regression may or may not take a pathological turn, but it most certainly will be accompanied by conflict, loss of responsibility, loss of initiative, and increased immaturity, together with a basic frustration that cannot help but hinder growth to perfection and impair apostolic efficiency and effectiveness. One cannot avoid the impression that much of the submissiveness and passivity that spiritual writers bemoan is due to this very loss of identity. Canon Leclercq has remarked on this point:

> The apostolate is thus a work of acquired perfection. A man will, in principle, consecrate himself to it in proportion as he is perfect. Imperfection tarnishes the

apostolate. Working in the Lord's service presupposes a soul pervaded by grace and dominated by love. Insofar as one is imperfect, one's actions will be vitiated by love of self; even preaching the word of God will be tainted, if the preacher is imperfect, for it will be mingled with self-love, with all that goes with it, vanity, seeking for prestige or for ease, fear of responsibilities, desire to please the powerful, etc. One can only teach the word of God exactly, in proportion as God is entirely master of one's soul, entirely free to accomplish His work through His servant, in proportion as one is emptied of self. But this is acquired perfection.[11]

7. Ascribed status versus achieved status.[12] The group tends to esteem or value those persons or factors that contribute to the group locomotion. In a situation where knowledge or ability was not held essential to the attainment of group goals, but where the primacy of value fell upon the organizational efficiency of the group, prestige and status tended to follow the lines of hierarchical structures of the group; precisely those in administrative positions not only were leaders in a formal sense, but also were contributing more effectively than the other members to the attainment of group goals. Where the professional fulfillment of specialized functions has become more and more essential to the attainment of group goals, the knowledgeability and

---

[11] J. Leclercq, *The Religious Vocation* (New York: P. J. Kenedy, 1955), p. 155.

[12] I am following Fichter's alignment of respective characteristics in discussing this characteristic of the professional or bureaucratic mode of organization (see fn. 7). The division of ascribed versus achieved status has a definite validity in discussing the religious organization, but not all authors agree that this characteristic adequately separates the professional from the bureaucratic type of organization. See also P. M. Blau and W. R. Scott, *Formal Organizations: A Comparative Approach* (San Francisco: Chandler, 1962) p. 61 *et passim*.

professional skill of individual members has been elevated by the group to a position of higher esteem and value.

The fact that a new hierarchy of status is imposed upon the preexisting hierarchy and that more often than not the individuals who hold high status in the respective hierarchies are different gives rise to a twofold influence upon the group culture that can, but need not, be a source of conflict. If interaction between the two status hierarchies is sufficiently flexible that intelligent cooperation is achieved, the two structures can operate in mutual support. The more stable and generally more influential status is the ascribed status of authority, precisely because it is part of the formalized structure of the organization that reinforces and supports it.

8. Service to the organization versus service to the client: It is difficult to say to what extent this characteristic has or has not been realized in religious groups. The difference in orientation lies in the fact that in the first instance the individual directly fulfills a function within the organization, and it is the organization that serves the public; in the second instance, the individual directly serves the public, and the organization exists in order to help the professional perform the function.

From an organizational point of view, service to the system would demand the priority of conformity and submission to directives of superiors. Service to the client would demand a greater reliance on personal judgment of individuals and on orientation more supervisory than directive. From the individual's point of view, service to the organization would place a premium on obedience and the avoidance of responsibility, whereas the second orientation would demand the acceptance of professional responsibilities and a willingness to take a stand on one's own abilities and knowledge rather than depend on the system for support.

As in other facets of the bureaucratic-professional tension, the resolution lies in the combination of certain aspects of both orientations. In certain circumstances the orientation of service to the client is primary and its prerogatives should be admitted; but there are undoubtedly other circumstances in which service to the system is to be preferred. In counseling on a marriage problem or in directing a penitent, the religious priest is immediately concerned with his professional service to his client. But in certain phases of his community-centered activity, such as attendance at choir, his primary orientation is toward service of the community or, more explicitly, service of God in and through the community. In the services that are directly professional it is clear that the religious must function as a professional person. Consequently, the individual's resolution of this tension must be subject to his personal prudential judgment to a much greater extent than if the tension in service orientation did not exist.

The tendency of a member of a group to exercise initiative is determined not only by group pressures or structural characteristics, but also by characteristics of the individual himself. For example, it has been found that greater participation in efforts to achieve a goal is manifested by members who are more confident of their own views.[13] It seems quite clear that persons with

---

[13] J. R. P. French and R. Snyder, "Leadership and Interpersonal Power," in D. Cartwright, ed., *Studies in Social Power* (Ann Arbor, Mich.: Institute for Social Research, 1959).

weak opinions are more vulnerable to contrary group pressures.[14] Persons who show a high degree of initiative also manifest a high degree of ego strength[15] and a high need for achievement.

Such findings seem to indicate that initiative is related to maturity and strength of personality and high motivation. Confidence in one's ability to perform well depends on past experiences of success or failure in task performance in comparison with group standards of success or failure. An individual may possess a potential for high level performance that is not manifested because previous group evaluations have been negative or restrictive. Children who are not regarded highly by parents and friends tend to evaluate themselves poorly,[16] and extreme conformists tend to perceive their parents as harsh, punitive, restricting, and rejecting more frequently than independent persons.[17]

These findings suggest that the conforming person has a poorly developed sense of his own worth, which derives from the implicit or explicit devaluation of his activities within his immediate and significant (to him) social environment. The most serious and far-reaching devaluation would occur at the hands of a rejecting parent. Not only does the conformist tend to be lacking in self-esteem, but also he is left with an intensified

[14] D. Cartwright and A. Zander, "Group Pressures and Group Standards," in Cartwright and Zander, *op. cit.*, p. 176.

[15] E. J. Thomas, "Effects of Role Interdependence and Ego-Strength on Group Functioning" (doctoral dissertation, University of Michigan, 1956).

[16] P. S. Sears, "Level of Aspiration in Relation to Some Variables of Personality: Clinical Studies, *Journal of Social Psychology*, XIV (1941), 311-36.

[17] P. H. Mussen and J. Kagan, "Group Conformity and Perceptions of Parents, *Child Development*, XXIX (1958), 57-60.

need for social approval. Experimental evidence seems to support the view that individuals with high social-approval and low self-approval motivation yield to the influence of the majority much more readily than individuals with the opposite characteristics of low social-approval and high self-approval motivation.[18] Significant for the religious group is the fact that the tendency for the conforming person to conform is even greater when the norm is represented by an authority figure than when the norm is the judgment of the majority.[19] It would be reasonable to expect the conforming type of person to be very strongly influenced in the bureaucratic structure of the religious group.

The significant point in the consideration of individual characteristics is that traits of low self-esteem, intensified need for social approval, lack of self-confidence, and so forth derive from the interaction of the individual within his significant social environment. Although interaction within the family environment is a decisive influence in shaping the personality of the child, personality growth does not stop at the end of childhood years. The identity crisis does not come until the adolescent years;[20] thus the process of interaction with significant social groups must be extended into the adult years.

---

[18] G. Moeller and M. H. Appelzweig, "A Motivational Factor in Conformity," *Journal of Abnormal and Social Psychology,* LV (1957), 114-20.

[19] A. S. Luchins and E. H. Luchins, "On Conformity with Judgments of a Majority or an Authority," *Journal of Social Psychology,* LIII (1961), 303-16.

[20] E. H. Erikson, *Identity and the Life Cycle* (New York: International Universities Press, 1959), pp. 101-64.

We have already seen that the influences that reinforce depersonalization—ritualization and the reduction
of personal responsibility—affect the individual personality in the form of a regressive loss of identity. There
is the danger that the candidate who comes to the religious life in his adolescent years (that is to say, in the
years in which he can be expected to pass through the
basic crisis of identity formation) will be subjected to
influences that undermine the natural growth to personal maturity and will cultivate his less mature needs
to conform. His sense of identification with the group
will be fixed in terms of the standards of conformity
generated by the group, and most especially by the authority figures who direct his formation and control the
functions of the group.

As a final word on this most complex and important
subject, I would like to observe that the high premium
placed on creativity, productivity, and initiative in our
society makes it increasingly imperative that religious
functionaries demonstrate these qualities over the wide
range of their apostolic and professional activities. In
an earlier period, when the demand was neither so
widespread nor so intense, the religious group could
be satisfied with a statistical assurance that some of
the stronger egos among its membership would demonstrate enough creativity and productivity to carry the
load for the group.

That assurance is rapidly diminishing in our time, so
that the religious group can no longer rely on chance
factors to give it outstanding workers. There is a pressing need to eliminate practices that are obvious hin-
drances to personal growth and maturity among mem-

bers, and the group must realistically search for better means to foster that growth and increase apostolic effectiveness on all levels, both spiritual and professional. It is the lesson of our spiritual tradition that the immature religious can be neither spiritually mature nor professionally responsible.

With profound insight, Leclercq has written in regard to apostolic responsibility: "An apostle must have the courage to undertake responsibilities. This courage will produce initiative. An apostle must be bold and daring."[21] I would like to add to this a correlative observation: the superior must have the courage to permit his members to undertake responsibilities. This courage will also produce initiative. The superior too must be bold and daring.

---

[21] Leclercq, *op. cit.*, p. 165.

6

Leadership in the
Religious Community

At several points in this study, we have touched tangentially on the relations between the religious superior and his members. We do not intend to repeat here the discussion of the religious superior's function but rather to focus on his role as leader of the religious group. Although the bases of social power may be widely distributed in the group, the influence of the superior remains the single most important factor, and its significance must not be underestimated.

A tremendous amount of energy has been expended on the study of the problem of leadership, but unfortunately the energy has produced less light than heat. The major approaches to this problem have concentrated either on the study of traits or on the interaction of the leader with other members of his group. According to the older trait approach, the leader was considered the kind of personality who would assume a position of dominance in a variety of social situations. Study of leadership thus became an attempt to identify the personality factors characteristic of such individuals. The difficulty was that the same person did not always lead in every situation. Adherents of the trait approach were consequently forced to shift their ground a little and focus on the traits that characterized the leader in each kind of situation.

The limitations of this approach persuaded many students to consider other possible reasons for emergence of the leader. Eventually, it was recognized that a leader's emergence hinged not only on his personality traits, but also on his interaction with other members of the group who must accept or reject his leadership. The range of variables that had to be considered was broadened, but in an interactional framework it became understandable why individuals with leadership traits were often not designated as leaders by a group or why the group accepted one leader in one type of situation and another in another. Current research on the concept of leadership is conducted almost exclusively within this interactional framework.

There seems to be general agreement that, whatever else it may be, leadership is a group phenomenon and that the concept of leader applies to the activities of members who exercise a significant influence on the group. As we have seen, every member of the group has an influence on the group culture, and depending on the criteria of influence, nearly every member can be differentiated from the others in that he exercises a significant influence in terms of this one isolated criterion. Some students of leadership have concluded that any member of the group can and does exhibit some degree of leadership.[1] In this approach, the concept of leader becomes so diluted that it is relatively meaning-

---

[1] B. M. Bass, *Leadership, Psychology, and Organizational Behavior* (New York: Harper, 1960).

less and does not seem to differ very much from the concept of member.

The notion of leadership has consequently been linked more closely to the exercise of power,[2] that is, the ability to influence other members of the group to change their behavior. But leadership is not just *any* power-relation; it depends, rather, on the recognition by other members of the group that the leader may legitimately prescribe patterns of behavior for the group to follow.

It is possible to distinguish several bases of social power:[3] (1) *reward power,* which is based on the member's perception that others have the ability to reward his behavior; (2) *coercive power,* which is based on the perception that others can punish his behavior; (3) *legitimate power,* which is based on the perception that others have a legitimate right to direct his behavior; (4) *referent power,* which is based on the member's identification with others; and (5)*expert power,* which is based on the recognition of special knowledge or expertness in the other. The exercise of leadership is directly related to the exercise of legitimate power; yet, although our main concern will be with legitimate power, the function of the leader does not exclude other power relations.

French and Raven[4] formulate several hypotheses concerning these bases of social power:

---

[2] K. F. Janda, "Towards the Explication of the Concept of Leadership in Terms of the Concept of Power," *Human Relations,* XIII (1960), 345-63.

[3] J. R. P. French, Jr. and B. Raven, "The Bases of Social Power," in D. Cartwright, ed., *Studies in Social Power* (Ann Arbor, Mich.: Institute for Social Research, 1959), pp. 150-67.

[4] *Ibid.*

1. For all types of social power, the stronger the power's basis, the greater the power will be. It is important to remember that the basis of power rests on the perception of the group or of any of the members of the group that the leader has this or that quality. It is not enough, for example, that a person have expert knowledge in order that he exercise expert power; it is necessary that the group recognize him as possessing that knowledge and therefore accept him as an expert.

2. The range of activities within which any type of power can be exercised will vary greatly. In general, referent power will have the broadest range. That is to say, the range of activities that can be affected or changed by reason of the individual member's identification with the leader or (as is often true in religious groups) with the group itself is broader than that of any other basis of power. This observation lends weight to our previous remarks on the importance of the identification process for the functioning of the religious group (see Chapter 4).

3. Any attempt to utilize power outside its range will tend toward its reduction. This is important, because it means that when the superior exerts power on the group beyond the range of that power, he is reducing by a like amount the basis of his capacity to influence the group. This is obvious in the use of expert power: if the expert tries to use his special power to influence the group in an area where he exceeds his competence, he will engender in the group a tendency to disregard even his expert opinion.

In the exercise of legitimate power, the superior can overstep the bounds of his legitimate authority. The range of his authority is established by the formal structure of the religious organization, but informal group norms of legitimacy are also in operation. In general, subject to the formal norms of the distribution of authority, the group evolves its own standard of what the superior can or cannot legitimately demand. If the superior exceeds the limit established by the group's informal consensus, he will, to an equal degree, be exceeding the range of his legitimate power. He thereby reduces the power itself (since the basis of legitimate power is the group's perception of the legitimacy of his exercise of authority.

Deviation in interpreting the formal norms of the exercise of legitimate authority is more likely true of the superior than of the group, since his individual judgment is more liable to be inaccurate than the group judgment and since he is open to the temptation to exercise his role as superior in all areas. In the properly functioning community, these tendencies are minimized by accurate feedback and open communication between superior and members.

4. A new state of the group system produced by the influence of reward or coercive power will be highly dependent on the agent exercising the power, and the more observable the conformity of the members, the more dependent the new state will be. In the other three types of power, the new state is dependent in the beginning, but the level of observability has no effect on the degree of dependence. Consequently, if the superior tries to enforce external conformity by a system of rewards and/or punishments, external conformity will depend on his continued exercise of this type of power. Members will conform as long as he rewards or punishes. However, influence exerted on the group by

the superior in virtue of his legitimate power (as an example) would not be subject to his limitation. Often when a system of rewards and punishments (usually a very subtle system) has been implemented in houses of formation, external conformity in observable behavior has been achieved. All too frequently, however, it has been achieved at the cost of those internalized values that are the substance of religious life.

5. Coercion results in decreased attraction and high resistance of the member to the leader; reward results in increased attraction and low resistance.

6. The more legitimate the coercion, the less it will produce resistance and decreased attraction. In this case, legitimate power is joined to coercive power and mitigates the effects of the latter.

Our primary concern in the relation between superior and member is with legitimate power. Such power may be based on cultural values which specify that a member possessing certain characteristics has the right to prescribe behavior for the others who do not have these characteristics; or, legitimate power may be founded on the acceptance of the social structure, in the sense that if a group's social structure involves a hierarchy of authority, members who accept such a structure will also accept the legitimate authority of those holding superior offices in that hierarchy; or again, legitimate power can arise by virtue of designation by a legitimizing agent, as in the designation of a local superior by higher authority or in the appointment of an individual to a special office not included in the preexistent hierarchy.[5] It is these last two bases of legitimate power that are

---

[5] *Ibid.*

most important in more or less permanent groups such as the religious group .

Experimental evidence has demonstrated that the amount and the effectiveness of the legitimate power exercised by a leader depends on the degree to which the leader is accepted as such by the rest of the group.[6] Raven and French[7] used a situation in which a supervisor of one group was represented as having group support through election and the supervisor of a second group took over her position without group support. Coercion was introduced by levying a monetary fine on half the members in each group for nonconformity.

The results indicate that where group support was obtained, there was greater acceptance of the legitimacy of the supervisor's office, greater justification in the group for the supervisor's behavior, greater personal attraction between individual workers and the supervisor, and a higher degree of private acceptance of the supervisor's influence. The introduction of coercion neither increased public conformity nor lessened the degree of legitimacy. When the leader is elected, there is great probability, at least in a democratic society, that he will be accepted by the group as having a right to exercise legitimate power.[8] Here the group itself serves as the legitimizing agent giving one individual authority over the rest of the group.

---

[6] J. R. P. French, Jr. and R. Snyder, "Leadership and Interpersonal Power," in Cartwright, op. cit., pp. 118-49.

[7] B. H. Raven and J. R. P. French, Jr., "Legitimate Power, Coercive Power, and Observability in Social Influence," Sociometry, XXI (1958), 83-97.

[8] B. H. Raven and J. R. P. French, Jr., "Group Support, Legitimate Power, and Social Influence," Journal of Personality, XXVI (1958), 400-09.

Only occasionally does the religious group choose its superiors by an elective process; usually the superior is appointed by a higher authority in the hierarchical structure of the group. The basis of legitimate power lies essentially in the acceptance of the social structure of the organization by the members. This, of course, depends on the forces of attraction to the group and group participation, which we have discussed (see Chapter 3).

The notion of legitimate power that has traditionally evolved in religious groups has a very special character. By the vow of obedience that every religious must pronounce, he binds himself to obey all commands imposed on him by the legitimate superior in virtue of the vow under the penalty of grave sin. The superior is thus regarded as taking the place of God, so that his commands represent God's will to the member. This emphasis undoubtedly reflects the idea that all authority derives ultimately from God. The superior, in exercising legitimate authority within the legal framework of his institute and the canonical prescriptions of the Church, is derivatively exercising God's authority.

This framework for the consideration of authority places powerful stress on the element of legitimacy and tends to bring basic motivations to bear in insuring group support of the superior. The more the superior is accepted and the more influence he wields because of this emphasis on legitimacy, the greater the risk of overemphasizing conformity and repressing initiative. Thus, it is well for the superior to keep in mind the theological caution urged by Father Rahner:[9]

---

[9] K. Rahner, "A Basic Ignatian Concept: Some Reflections on Obedience," *Woodstock Letters*, LXXXVI (1957), 291-310.

> If the subject must obey in order not to be disobedient before God, this fact is no proof that the command given was the command which, according to God's antecedent will, should have been given. It can be the product of a permitted fault in the superior. It can proceed from dead traditionalism, from human limitations, from routine, from a shortsighted system of uniformism, from a lack of imagination, and from many other factors.

The critical concern in considering religious authority (within the limitations of this study) is not the theological derivation of the authority that the superior exercises. It is rather, on the one hand, the superior's perception of his own authoritative position and, on the other hand, the member's perception of his authoritative position. If the superior exercises his God-given authority as if his mandate bore with it a charism of inerrancy, his action can have devastating repressive effects on the group and will inevitably inhibit the feedback and communication processes that are so vital to group functioning. The result for the members will be tendencies to shift responsibility to the superior and to fall into a pattern of irresponsibility, dependency, and lack of initiative.

It is a fairly well-established conclusion of experimental studies that the behavior of groups tends to differ markedly when they are under the influence of leaders who act differently.[10] Different kinds of work groups, for example, vary in their performances in accordance with the characteristic behavior of the supervisor. Supervisors of the more effective groups seemed

---

[10] R. White and R. Lippitt, "Leader Behavior and Member Reaction in Three 'Social Climates'," in D. Cartwright and A. Zander, eds., *Group Dynamics* (Evanston, Ill.: Row, Peterson, 1953), pp. 527-53.

better able to play more differentiated roles than supervisors of less effective groups. They spent more time in
planning what was to be done, in making sure the necessary materials were available, and in initiating the progressive steps in the work program. The more effective
supervisors seemed better able to delegate authority to
other members of the work group; they checked on
their subordinates less often and generally gave their
subordinates more encouragement and support than
did their less effective colleagues; and they were better
able to develop cohesiveness among their associates
than were the supervisors of groups with poorer performance.[11] Research finding of this nature led Likert[12]
to conclude that the effective leader

> . . . creates a good working team which has a friendly,
> cooperative atmosphere with high group loyalty. He
> seems to build this high group loyalty through using
> participation and other recognized methods of group
> leadership. Moreover, the work group under his leader-
> ship exercises influence upward upon organizational
> objectives, methods, etc., and in turn accepts as group
> goals those objectives which must be achieved if the
> group is to do its part of the total task of the organiza-
> tion effectively and at a high level of performance. . . .

The effectiveness of the leader is influenced by the
degree to which he is or is not liked by the group. For
example, not only do better-liked officers in the Air
Force try to influence their men more than less well-

[11] R. L. Kahn and D. Katz, "Leadership Practices in Relation to
Productivity and Morale," in Cartwright and Zander, *op. cit.*, pp.
554-70.
[12] R. Likert, "An Emerging Theory of Organization, Leadership and
Management," in L. Petrillo and B. M. Bass, eds., *Leadership and
Interpersonal Behavior* (New York: Holt, Rinehart and Winston,
1961).

liked officers, but they more often succeed in doing it.[13] But the picture is more complex than this simple finding would indicate. Using a somewhat different approach, Fiedler[14] has been able to show that the more effective leaders commonly maintain a greater "psychological distance" between themselves and their subordinates than do less effective leaders. This seems to support the common practice in military and industrial organizations of maintaining a certain distance between officers and troops and between company officials and workers.

Fiedler observes that these customs seem to influence group effectiveness, not because subordinates will not follow a leader with whom they are too familiar, but because the leader who is too close to his men may find it more difficult to reach objective decisions, influenced as he would be by his emotional involvements and relations with members of his group.[15] However, the types of groups that reflect increased effectiveness in a climate of social distance between leader and followers are primarily task-oriented. Psychologically distant leaders of task-oriented groups are more effective than leaders who encourage a warmer, psychologically closer relationship with their subordinates.

The reasons for this phenomenon are not altogether clear, but it has been suggested that close interpersonal relations between superior and member make it difficult for the superior to administer discipline, or that the

---

[13] French and Snyder, "Leadership . . .," in Cartwright, *op. cit.*
[14] F. Fiedler, "The Leader's Psychological Distance and Group Effectiveness," in Cartwright and Zander, *op. cit.*, pp. 586-606.
[15] F. Fiedler, "A Note on Leadership Theory: The Effect of Social Barriers between Leaders and Followers," *Sociometry*, XX (1957), 87-94.

resulting emotional involvement may make the superior emotionally dependent on one or two group members and give rise to rivalries and favoritism. In any case, psychological distance seems to lead to better fulfillment of individual roles and functions by placing an emphasis on the task.[16] However, the religious group does not exist merely for the performance of a task.

Apparently the functions of effective leadership can be divided in terms of the basic dichotomy of tendencies that characterize the structure of any group, that is, the tendencies to emotionality or to work.[17] Bales[18] makes a parallel distinction between group problems involving goal achievement and adaptation to external demands and problems involving internal integration and the expression of emotional tensions. He calls the former set of problems "adaptive-instrumental," and their solution demands activity by the group in the task area (see chart, page 21). The second set are called "integrative-expressive," and for their solution activity in the emotional area is required.

Slater's[19] research in this area has made it clear that the differentiation of roles with respect to these distinct problem areas is a fundamental aspect of group functioning, particularly in small groups. Consequently, in the religious group, where the leader is appointed and where there is only one principal leader, he or she cannot be expected to fulfill both functions completely. The ideal superior would be sufficiently skillful and

---

[16] Fiedler, "A Note on Leadership Theory . . . ," *op. cit.*

[17] See discussion of Bion's work in Chapter 2.

[18] R. F. Bales, *Interaction Process Analysis* (Cambridge, Mass.: Addison-Wesley Press, 1951).

[19] P. E. Slater, "Role Differentiation in Small Groups," *American Sociological Review*, XX (1955), 300-10.

flexible to handle both aspects of group functioning; he would effectively channel group efforts to achieve group goals and at the same time respond sympathetically to individual needs of group members.

Such men are rare, as Slater[20] has pointed out, for both sociological and psychological reasons. Sociologically, task and emotional roles are not compatible; adaptation to pressures from outside the group (task-orientation) forces a continual readjustment of the group's internal structure, and this inevitably involves shifts in attitudes, values, emotional attachments, and so on, of individual members. On the other hand, concern with the internal social-emotional problems tends to support dominant values and attitudes of members. As a result, the activity of the task-oriented leader usually produces negative feelings among members of the group, depending on the extent to which the group is or is not emotionally oriented. When task-orientation and cohesiveness are high, these feelings are minimized, but when they are low, negative feelings may be expressed in outright dislike. Psychologically, the leader may be predisposed to assume a particular role; for the well-liked emotional leader, avoidance of conflict may be a felt necessity, so that he avoids disharmony and tries to maintain a harmonious mediocrity. He may even avoid task functions because of their inherent threat to him.

Or the task-oriented leader may assume his role because of an unwillingness to respond to the needs of other members, an unwillingness arising out of his own anxiety over participation in close interpersonal rela-

---

20 *Ibid.*

tions and emotional involvements. For example, the leader of a task-oriented group may not only find social distance a more effective way for the group to go about its business, but also because of his own personal needs it may serve as the more congenial way of operating.

The tendency for a leader's role functioning to differentiate reflects a certain amount of inflexibility or lack of capacity in the leader. The extent to which he is dominated by one or another set of personal needs contributes to his inability to meet the opposing set of group problems. Likewise, the effectiveness of his functioning will depend in great degree on the balance of the group's basic tendencies. Applying this observation to the religious group, the functioning of the superior who follows one orientation more than another because of the pressure of personal needs will be affected for better or worse by the corresponding balance of his community's tendencies to work or emotionality.

The superior who tends to an emotional orientation may get along very well with a strongly emotion-oriented group, but task functions may suffer as a result. Similarly, the strongly task-oriented superior may have great success with a task-oriented group, but the inner life of the community and the satisfaction of its members' individual needs may suffer. Another damaging situation can be envisioned when the types are crossed, when, for example, a task-oriented superior is placed in charge of an emotionally-oriented group, or conversely, an emotionally-oriented superior is named to head a task-oriented group. Conflict and frustration are bound to be produced. It is little wonder that the traditional picture of the ideal religious superior has been painted to emphasize high capacity to perform successfully both

in task performance and in responsiveness to the emotional needs of the inner system of the group and its
members.[21]

The successful religious superior must, in the final
analysis, be a psychologically mature individual who
has been able to attain a secure sense of his own identity. He is able to accept responsibility, act effectively to
attain specific goals, and relate maturely and objectively
with his superiors and with his subordinates—and do all
this without anxiety or a need to avoid personal psychological threat.

One must remember that the functioning of the superior is part of an interactional situation. The way a
superior acts and the characteristic positions he adopts
are a product of his own personality in interaction with
the dynamics of the group itself. By reason of the prestige and influence of his position, the superior can produce a strong effect on the group, but even as he attempts to influence the group he is being influenced
by it.

The very fact of his being placed in the superior's
position will affect his opinions. Experiments in which
workers were promoted to positions of responsibility
and leadership show that members so advanced under-
go a systematic alteration in attitudes; after advance-
ment to a position of leadership, they displayed significantly more positive attitudes toward the organization.[22]
The same phenomenon undoubtedly occurs in religious

---

[21] C. Aquaviva, "Effective Governing," *Review for Religious*, XIV
(1955), 235-40. This is a translation of a chapter from Aquaviva's
Industriae, a classic treatise on religious government.
[22] D. Cartwright and A. Zander, "Issues and Basic Assumptions," in
Cartwright and Zander, *op. cit.*, p. 50.

groups, and with the office of superior the tremendous prestige tends to intensify the effect. It would seem that in addition to superiors being chosen from members who show positive attitudes to the organization, the social position of the office itself helps modify superiors' attitudes so that they become even more positive. The extent to which the superior's positive attitudes become rigidly conformist depends in large measure on his own maturity and capacity for independent judgment. But at the same time, he is undoubtedly influenced by the role expectations inherent in the culture of the group.

When social-defense mechanisms become a significant aspect of the inner life of the group (see Chapter 4), the group's influence can be very strong, even though unconscious. If the superior does not feel secure in his own exercise of responsibility, a self-reinforcing social-defense system will be set up in the group that will be detrimental both to the effectiveness of the superior's leadership and to the solution of the group's needs.

Granted the maturity and the secure functioning of the superior, a mutual adaptation between superior and group is necessary to bring about the modifications in group culture that will insure effective group functioning. Every group presents a balance of tendencies to work or emotionality that must inevitably be readjusted and modified by the introduction of a new superior. The superior exercises a strong influence on the group through his prestige and authority, and the impact of each superior will be unique. Within the group discrepancies arise that are accompanied by strain; strain reduction through communication follows as a natural consequence (see Chapter 2).

From the superior's point of view, a feedback process is set up that enables him to gauge the balance of tendencies in the group, to read its basic assumptions, to understand the impact of the group culture, and to receive information about his personal impact on these various facets of group life. We have considered at length the nature and importance of feedback and communication in the continued adjustment by which the group maintains itself under shifting external and internal conditions (see Chapter 2).

Factors in the superior-member relation can work to interfere with effective feedback. There is a general tendency for group members to reduce psychological distance between themselves and more powerful members and to increase the distance to the less powerful members. The former tendency increases when the psychological distance is small, the latter increases with the increase of distance. However, if the initial distance between the ordinary members and the more powerful members is too great, the preference decreases.[23] There is also a corresponding decrease in communicative behavior, which is seemingly linked to the phenomenon of "social distance." Consequently, if the initial distance between superior and members is too great, there will be a tendency for the distance to be preserved. Although this sort of distance seems to be effective in strictly task-oriented groups, it is doubtful that it would be serviceable to the religious group.

---

23 M. Mulder, "The Power Variable in Communication Experiments," *Human Relations*, XIII (1960), 241-57.

The very fact that a group is structured hierarchically seems to set up restraints against free communication, particularly in the communication of criticism or hostility from the lower to the higher level.[24] As a result, a certain selectivity may be expected in the information fed back to the superior. Pleasant matters are more likely to be communicated than unpleasant, achievements rather than failures; anything that reflects negatively on the competence and security of members at the lower level is likely to be screened out. The tendency to maximize positive aspects of performance and minimize negative aspects will increase in direct proportion to the strength of the upward-mobility aspirations among members at the lower level. Members may thus be unconsciously (or even consciously) influenced to hide their failures, problems, and difficulties from the superior; yet it is precisely these matters that are of the greatest importance to the superior's effective governing.

The two principal modifying influences in this situation stem from the member's trust of the superior's motives and intentions and from his perception of the superior's degree of influence over the member's potential mobility in the organization. The disruption of communication will be greatest under conditions of high aspiration in the member, a low degree of trust between member and superior, and the member's perception of the superior as highly influential.[25] To a cer-

---

[24] L. Festinger, "Informal Social Communication," *Psychological Review*, LVII (1950), 271-82. See also W. H. Read, "Upward Communication in Industrial Hierarchies," *Human Relations,* XV (1962), 3-15.
[25] Read, "Upward Communication . . . ," *op. cit.*

tain extent, the religious member, particularly during his early years of formation but also in the later years of his life, usually sees the superior as possessing considerable influence over what he can or cannot do. This is for the most part a realistic perception, since in fact the superior's permission is required for practically all phases of the religious' life. Even more than the question of this or that particular activity is the question of the underlying need of the member for the superior's, esteem and approbation.

These aspects of the superior-member relation can effectively sever communication from member to superior unless the relationship is dominated by trust. We have already considered the relationship between trust and communication (see Chapter 2). The necessity of trust, however, is emphasized when placed in the context of mechanisms that tend to interfere with effective communications between the various levels of the group structure.

The leader can adopt one of several general modes of behavior in relation to the group, each of which seems to have definite implications for group functioning. Each such "social climate" seems to be associated with a pattern of characteristics. White and Lippitt[26] have summarized some of the results of their research in terms of three social climates; autocratic, democratic, and laissez-faire.[27] They found that the reactions to each climate are quite different and that the reaction to autocracy usually has two forms, dependent and aggressive. The major findings can be summarized as follows:

---

[26] White and Lippitt, "Leader Behavior . . .," *op. cit.*
[27] R. White and R. Lippitt, *Autocracy and Democracy: An Experimental Inquiry* (New York: Harper, 1960).

1. There were a large number of leader-dependent actions in both reactions to autocracy.

2. There was a large amount of critical discontent and aggressive behavior in the aggressive reaction to autocracy.

3. Friendly and confiding conversation and group-minded suggestions were frequent in the democratic group.

4. The democratic and laissez-faire groups differed in the amount of open-minded conversation.

5. There was a large difference between the two reactions to autocracy in the amount of aggressive behavior, while the democratic and laissez-faire groups were intermediate in this regard.

6. The subdued atmosphere in the submissive reaction to autocracy was reflected in the small total of aggressive behavior, attention demands, group-minded suggestions, and play-minded remarks.

7. The proportion of group-minded suggestions was small in both autocratic reactions, but very large in the laissez-faire group.

8. Laissez-faire differed from democracy in that there was less work and poorer work and a greater tendency to play.

9. The democratic orientation can be efficient, although the quantity of work done in the autocratic group was greater.

10. Work motivation was greater in the democratic group, as shown by the tendency to keep working when the leader left the room.

11. The democratic group showed more originality.

12. Autocracy can create much hostility and aggression, which are reflected in more dominating ascendance, much greater hostility, more demands for attention, greater destructiveness and scapegoat behavior.

13. Autocracy can create discontent that does not appear on the surface, as indicated by dropouts, greater expression of discontent even when the general reaction is submissive, and "release behavior" suggesting the existence of previous frustration.

14. There was more dependence and less individuality in the autocratic group.

15. There was more group-mindedness and friendliness in the democratic group.

16. There was a greater tendency for formation of in-group and out-group divisions in the authoritarian group than in the democratic group.

Although these classic studies were conducted on boys' clubs, it seems reasonable to consider them as characteristic of the type of leadership in each situation. The authoritarian approach tends to emphasize bureaucratic values, with their consequences of lack of initiative, dependence, and poor motivation in the subjects. The defense of authoritarianism on the grounds of efficiency needs to be reexamined in more careful studies. A recent extensive review of experimental studies of authoritarian versus democratic leadership concludes that neither type of leadership has been shown to be consistently related to greater productivity.[28] The adoption of an authoritarian stance by a

---

[28] R. C. Anderson, "Learning in Discussions: A Resume of the Authoritarian-Democratic Studies," *Harvard Educational Review,* XXIX (1959), 201-15.

leader may be a reflection of immature emotional needs operating within the group, but the leader's response (that is, failure to modify group needs to a more mature and nondependent status) seems to suggest reciprocal needs in the leader for his or her authoritarian position. This type of adaptation is common enough for Erich Fromm to describe it in terms of "irrational authority," based on the need to have power over other people. The exercise of irrational authority is more often than not an attempt to escape anxiety, and it is paralleled by a reciprocal submission that Fromm describes in terms of a sado-masochistic orientation he calls the "authoritarian character structure."[29]

The authoritarian leader reduces his anxiety by dominating and controlling the lives of others, while the authoritarian character, in its submission to the authoritarian leader, finds the certainty and security it lacks within itself. From Fromm's intrapsychic point of view, this situation represents an interaction and mutual reinforcement of preexistent personality constellations. But it should be added that such an interrelation can be *produced* by the group interaction. The authoritarianism of the leader and the submission of the members can be regarded as a product of group-individual interaction. Consequently, the insecure person who is placed in a position of leadership may assume an authoritarian stance, even though there were no previous indications of such an inclination, because of the implicit and unconscious emotional demands within the group for dependency on the leader. In either supposition, an authoritarian stance by the leader reflects a basic lack of identity and maturity.

---

[29] E. Fromm, *Man for Himself* (New York: Rinehart, 1947).

Although an authoritarian stance obtains a certain reduction of anxiety, it does so at the cost of group initiative, responsibility, maturity, and the like. On the other hand, it is difficult for the leader of any group to trust his subordinates and have confidence in their competence to carry out relevant tasks while there is a certain amount of indeterminacy and uncertainty regarding the outcome. Experimentally, the leader who is willing to take the risk and assume responsibility for group action under such circumstances seems to be a person who is both relatively unconcerned about his nonconformity with group opinions and also more highly motivated.[30] Even so, the risk is well worth taking if it results in the more responsible, congenial, mature, and initiative-tolerating atmosphere of the more democratic group.

The problem that continually confronts every functioning group is that of adaptation, which of course implies change. The authoritarian imposition of change would undoubtedly be the most efficient way of achieving it rapidly within the group, if it were not for hostile and aggressive reactions it generates or (in the submissive type of reaction delineated by White and Lippitt[31]) for the submission and dependency (with their correlates of lack of responsibility and initiative) that it can elicit. The internal resistances of the group can make a shambles of the best-conceived and best-executed plans of its leaders.

---

[30] R. C. Ziller, "Leader Acceptance of Responsibility for Group Action under Conditions of Uncertainty and Risk," *Journal of Psychology*, XLVII (1959), 57-66.

[31] White and Lippitt, *Autocracy and Democracy, op. cit.*

The classic experiment along these lines was the work of Coch and French[32] who divided their experimental groups into three categories on the basis of the degree of participation of workers in planning changes in methods of work. Different groups of workers attended group meetings with management to discuss the problems involved in the contemplated changes. One group was not permitted any participation. A second group was permitted partial participation through specially trained operators from the group. The third and fourth groups were permitted total participation. The results of the experiment indicated a direct and positive relation between the amount of participation and the success of the shift from one work method to another. Evidently, the introduction of new methods had made employees feel insecure, caused them to worry over the effect of new piece-rates on their pay checks, and stirred up resentment against interference by management. As a result, informal group standards were set up to restrict the level of production.

With the introduction of participation, the situation was entirely changed psychologically. Workers were given the opportunity to take a responsible part in both the planning and the execution of changes; they were given the chance to exercise a certain amount of initiative and to develop a sense of involvement and identification with the success or lack of success of the new methods; internal resistances to an authoritarian management imposing changes from without petered out because this had, in fact, been eliminated and the work-

[32] L. Coch and J. R. P. French, Jr., "Overcoming Resistance to Change," *Human Relations*, I (1948), 512-32.

ers themselves had acted as the agents of change. A replication of this classic experiment was conducted in a Norwegian factory with the addition of better controls.[33] The results of the second experiment suggested that increased participation has a positive effect on production, labor-management relations, and job satisfaction only to the extent that certain conditions were present: that the decisions to be made were important; that the content of the decisions was relevant to the issue; that the participation was considered legitimate; and that there was no resistance on the part of the group to the methods for managing the change.

There is a general misapprehension that decision-making and giving orders are equivalent activities, but the fact is that decision-making is a much broader area than that of issuing orders. Fichter breaks the activity of authority into four steps: recognition of a problem, analysis of alternatives, choice of one alternative, and the executive order putting this choice into effect. The first three steps are preliminary to the exercise of authority, and it is not until the fourth step that legitimate authority is called into play.[34]

In our rapid sociocultural evolution, the complexities of problems in the constant and inevitable adaptation of the religious group cannot be faced or solved by any single person. The religious group does possess a residue

---

[33] J. R. P. French, Jr., J. Israel, and D. Aos, "An Experiment on Participation in a Norwegian Factory: Interpersonal Dimensions of Decision-Making," *Human Relations,* XIII (1960), 3-19.

[34] J. H. Fichter, S.J., "The Sociological Aspects of the Role of Authority in the Adaptation of the Religious Community for the Apostolate," in Joseph E. Haley, C.S.C., ed., *1958 Sisters' Institute of Spirituality* (Notre Dame, Ind.: University of Notre Dame Press, 1959), pp. 70-71.

of skill and technical information that can be placed at the service of the group. Father Rahner rightly emphasizes the altered function of the office of advisor or consultor to the superior, which is a proviso of canon law itself.[35] Now more than ever the superior needs expert advice and guidance to do justice to the responsibilities of his office. It is the function of the superior to require the mobilization of all the available resources of the community toward the achievement of goals for which the group exists. The superior should be able, therefore, to expand the area of responsible functioning to involve in one way or another, to one degree or another, all of his members.

To do this demands courage and strength of conviction in the superior. In the traditional conception of the superior-member relation, he is still regarded as the "pater familias," whose authority within his unit of jurisdiction is absolute and whose responsibility is total. Whether or not the superior broadens the exercise of responsibility in his community, he ultimately bears its burdens; if any egregious failures occur, he will have to bear the responsibility for the failure of the group. It requires real strength to accept this responsibility and at the same time not succumb to it.

Regardless of the formal structure of authority within the group, every superior has the option of creating an atmosphere of cooperation and responsible participation in his group or of creating an atmosphere of dependence and submission to authority. If he invites the contributions of his community at every level in which it is possible for a member to contribute (the prelimi-

---

[35] Rahner, "A Basic Ignatian Concept," *op. cit.*, p. 294.

nary steps of recognition, analysis, and decision), he can create an atmosphere that is essentially democratic. At the same time, there is no need to violate the formal structure of authority, since he alone, in virtue of his office as superior, has the power to give the executive order.

The traditional conceptualization of the religious group as a family, in which the superior is cast in the role of parent and the members in the role of children, tends to foster a kind of paternalism that is little more than a soft-sell authoritarianism. When paternalism is mixed with gentleness and "understanding" (the mother-knows-best kind of understanding), the effect can be to foster dependence and infantilism while muting the hostility and aggression that authoritarianism tends to generate. Hostile emotions are repressed rather than subdued, with the result that tension, conflict, and frustration are generated whenever the member cannot reduce himself or herself to the expected infantility.

In our time the office of superior is more demanding, requires greater intelligence and virtue, and has further reaching consequences than at any previous time in the history of religious life. The increased and complex demands placed on the religious group are inevitably transferred to the increasingly complex office of the religious superior. And, as Father Rahner has pointed out,[36] the likelihood that the superior will fail in his responsibilities is greater by reason of this intensification of demand.

The truly effective superior should be able to mobilize the resources of his community to support rather

[36] *Ibid.*

than conflict with his leadership. He must be capable of activating his community to a high level of perform-ance in the service of God's kingdom by all the devices of leadership—by stimulation and encouragement, by participation and broadened exercise of responsibility, by positive motivation and persuasion, by discipline and correction when necessary, by intelligence and pru-dence in his decisions and setting of objectives, and by communication of the noble ideals of religious life and religious perfection both in his words and in the tenor of his life. At the same time, he must participate in the internal life of the community, responding, guiding, helping, opening to each member of his community the opportunity and encouragement to grow in maturity, in self-fulfillment, and in the realization of the true independence and freedom of spirit in religious perfec-tion.

Perhaps this is too much to expect of any one fallible and limited man or woman, but the religious superior has assumed his trust from God, Who does not fail to support his burdens with the strength of His grace. If the superior tries to take the whole burden of responsi-bility upon himself and carry it on his own shoulders, he makes himself a superior with a community as part of his burden. If, however, he encourages and seeks the help of other members of the group in carrying out the functions and responsibilities involved in running the organization, he makes himself a superior with a com-munity that shares a part of his burden. The choice can often spell the difference between effective or ineffec-tive government, between the successful or unsuccessful realization of the goals of the religious group, and between the growth to religious maturity or the failure of religious vocation of the individual member of the religious group.

SUBJECT INDEX

A

Acting-out, 23, 24
Adaptation
  and authority, 127
  and group motivation, 130, 131
  for professional tasks, vii-x
Anxiety
  and authoritarian stance, 173
  and decision-making, 135, 138
  and group participation, 53
  and responsibility, 138
Authority
  and adaptation, 127
  and professionalism, 135
  in religious community, 133

B

Bargaining, 31, 32, 33
Basic assumptions, 19
  change, 25
  and emotionality, 20, 116
  in group process, 23, 25, 167
Bureaucratic orientation
  conformity, 148
  effects, 130
  efficiency, 128
  group, 2, 3, 11
  individual, 128
  initiative, 128
  intimacy, 6
  leadership, 131-133
  legalistic, 134
  organization, 127-129
  qualities, 128
  in religious community, 9, 11, 80-82
  rules, 128, 134
  size, 4, 5
  status, 128
  strict observance, 134
  structure, 141

C

Centralization, 70
Change
  authority, 173
  in basic assumption, 25
  conscious, 18, 19
  in group goals, 27
  unconscious, 18, 19
Charity, 66
Coalition, 31, 32, 33
Cognitive dissonance, 101-107
Cohesiveness
  attraction to group, 46, 67
  communication, 45-46, 96-98
  definition, 46
  group prestige, 67
  member's influence, 68
  productivity, 70
  in religious group, 75
Communication
  attraction, 35, 39
  attractiveness of group, 48, 59
  cohesiveness, 45
  defective, 58
  degree of relevance, 45
  deviation, 49
  disequilibrium, 37
  feedback, 34
  forces to, 43-50
  group process, 36-50
  initiative, 137
  mechanisms in religious group, 34
  perceived discrepancy, 38, 41, 42, 45, 46
  pressure to uniformity, 44, 47
  reduction of strain, 42-44
  trust, 39, 42
Competition, 31, 33
Conformity, 98, 101, 103-107
  acceptance, 124

AUTHOR INDEX

Anderson, R. C., 171
Aos, D., 175
Appelzweig, M.H., 148
Aquaviva, C., 165
Aronson, E., 101, 103, 105, 107
Atelak, F., 63
Back, K., 63
Baker, F., 66
Bales, R.F., 20, 21, 162
Bass, B.M., 34, 152
Berkowitz, L., 52, 67, 124, 125
Bier, W.C., ix
Bion, W.R., 17, 19, 20, 22, 24, 82, 113, 116
Black, K., 101
Blau, P.M., 11, 144
Bose, S.K., 70
Brehm, J.W., 104
Carlsmith, J.M., 104
Cartwright, D., 4, 51, 57, 62, 71, 73, 86, 109, 119, 123, 140, 146, 147, 165
Coch, L., 174
Cohen, A.R., 104
Consalvi, C., 52, 126
Darley, J., 71
Deutsch, M., 67, 71, 73, 74, 108
De Young, K., 66
Dittes, J., 53, 60
Eisenhower, D.D., 44
Ellertson, N., 71, 86
Erikson, E.H., 74, 91, 110, 116, 148
Exline, R., 63
Festinger, L., 43, 44, 45, 68, 101, 103, 105, 168
Fichter, J.H., ix, 6, 11, 12, 79, 80, 127, 128, 130, 144, 175
Fiedler, F., 161, 162
Fleming, W.H., 104
French, J.R.P., 146, 153, 157, 161, 174, 175
Fromm, E., 172
Gallen, J.F., 28, 30, 80, 84, 104
Gerard, H.B., 108
Ghei, S., 66
Goldman, M., 73
Gregory, D., 71, 86
Grinker, R., 53
Gross, N., 71
Haley, J.E., ix, 6, 11, 12
Hammond, L.K., 73
Hartley, R.E., 100
Harvey, O.J., 52, 126
Havelin, A., 55
Hitler, A., 35
Hollander, E.P., 125
Homans, G.C., 17
Horwitz, M., 56, 63
Israel, J., 60, 175
Jackson, J.M., 55, 65, 124
Jander, K.F., 153
Jennings, H.H., 17
Kagen, J., 147
Kahn, R.L., 160
Katz, D., 160
Kincannon, J., 66
Larson, L., 63
Leclercq, J., 143, 144, 150
Lee, F., 63
Likert, R., 160, 161
Lippitt, R., 159, 169, 173
Loomis, J.L., 74
Luchins, A.S., 148
Luchins, E.H., 148
Macaulay, J.R., 52, 125
Madden, E.H., 73
Martin, W., 71
McBride, D., 71, 86
McEwen, W.J., 27, 31, 32
Menzies, I.E.P., 119
Mills, J., 107

187